Somerset Dreams

Rosn + Patrick
Best wishs
Carol

By
Carol V. Johnson

Illustrated by
Rebecca Dobson

AuthorHouse™ UK Ltd.
500 Avebury Boulevard
Central Milton Keynes, MK9 2BE
www.authorhouse.co.uk
Phone: 08001974150

First published by AuthorHouse 11/4/2011

ISBN: 978-1-4567-9012-7 (sc)

This book is printed on acid-free paper.

authorHOUSE®

Acknowledgments.

Many thanks to my parents, Noel and Theresa Johnson.

To Ann Turvey, for her intriguing English lessons.

Also to Rebecca Dobson, for her beautiful illustrations, and to Sinead Ni Riain, for her photography.

For Kevin, Aaron and Darryl.
May all of your dreams come true.

Sometimes when you stand face to face
with someone, you cannot see his face.

Mikhail Gorbachev

Chapter 1: Double Trouble

In the quiet village of Midsomer-Atte-Stoke, which nestled comfortably in the middle of rural Somerset, where the scenery was always beautiful and the dairy produce ever so delicious, strange things were happening.

Fifi, the white lop-eared rabbit had been stolen from her hutch, making her Human-Being pet, Gracie, cry. Charlie, the St. Bernard, was recuperating in Dr. Sortuite's hospital for Takoda, after contracting a mysterious illness. Gizmo, the plump black cat from 'The Country Café' had disappeared without a trace.

In general, Human-Being pets were acting very strangely. Storekeepers argued with each other. Politicians were fighting. The police were called out to droves of disorders. Human-Being offspring were behaving particularly badly both at home and at school.

The weather was also most peculiar. Ferocious gales and storms appeared at one moment, while icy hailstones and snow appeared at others. All came suddenly and with cruel severity, but cleared away into lovely, sunny days in a fraction of a second.

But most important to the Human-Being pets of Midsomer-Atte-Stoke, the local apple juice had been tainted purple!

One Takoda whose sleeping habits were not interrupted by the strange goings on, was Mischa.

Dozing lazily in her bed, Mischa opened one weary brown eye and closed it again. She decided it was not quite time to get up. Not that this was first thing in the morning. It was normal for this Shetland sheepdog to have three, four, or even five naps during the day.

Her soft golden brown fur rose up and down gently as she continued her dream. A very strange dream indeed, involving food. She licked her lips and smiled in her sleep. Ahead of her, separating the sheltie from her cosy red-checked, fleece-lined basket, stood a wall of raspberry ripple ice cream. If she wanted to have a nap, she was going to have to lick her way through the ice cream. 'Hmmm, so tasty.' No sooner had she done that, a banana flavoured wall of ice cream appeared. Mischa drooled and smiled in her sleep. This ice cream was so very delicious and must have been made of real bananas and extra rich Cornish clotted cream.

Suddenly, a light tapping sound distracted her. 'Ice cream doesn't tap, it melts.' She licked her lips and her tongue extended to her wet, black nose.

The tapping started again. Tap, tap. Tap-tap-tap.

Mischa gave a big, lazy yawn, stretched all four golden brown legs and wagged her bushy brown tail, which ended in a black and white tip. She really could not be bothered to walk, so she lethargically crawled from the kitchen to the French windows in the living room, which looked onto the back garden.

Chiko, the robin who lived at the bottom of the garden in one of Mrs Jennings' apple trees, was frantically rapping his beak against the glass. He chirped loudly and angrily. With his head cocked to one side, he hopped from one foot to the other and flapped his wings furiously.

He tapped on the window again. Mischa beat her tail in a frenzy and concentrated hard; but even when putting her head on one side, she just couldn't hear what the robin was saying. So she ambled lazily to the back door and howled at her Human-Being pet to be let out.

Mrs Jennings, a cuddly shaped middle-aged lady, wobbled down the stairs like a large, pink jelly. She had the roundest, kindest face Mischa had ever seen on a Human-Being pet; not at all like grumpy Mr Barrowclough from next door, who seemed to have been born with a frown welded onto his. Mrs Jennings' face was pink and always smiley, her cheeks adorning two red blobs, and looked very much like a rosy apple.

As usual, Mrs Jennings was wearing her pink blouse with a big bow at the collar, and a navy blue pinafore, which had a deep pocket. Inside this pocket, she always had a little something that was nice and tasty.

Mischa watched the pink fluffy slippers descend slowly down the worn carpet stairs. She yipped delightedly, sat on her hind legs and raised her front paws, panting and laughing for Mrs Jennings.

'Mischa, yer so spoiled' she said, rubbing the dog's head and popping a chunk of chocolate chip cookie into her eagerly awaiting mouth.

'Yes, I know that, Mrs. J.' woofed Mischa excitedly. 'But aren't I the sweetest, cutest dog in the world. Aren't you so glad that you have me to look after you? Aren't you? Aren't you?' She jumped up and down and chased her tail.

Mrs Jennings opened the back door and released Mischa into the large, sprawling, country garden.

'Goodness, Mischa, yer lazy pup' she said in her broad West Country accent. 'Oi didn't think you were ever goin' ta get up. You had yer breakfast and yer dinner then napped fer the rest of the time! Yer need a lot more exercise my dear girl. Off yer go and make sure you spend at least thirty minutes running around the lawn. Mind yer don't dig up me plants or me rhubarb. And don't come back with yer fur full of mud an' grass.'

Mischa smiled politely, wagged her tail and barked good-bye. She raced after Chiko, who had flown on ahead, and arrived at the rickety fence at the bottom of the garden. There she found Delia, a superbly groomed, sleek, majestic-looking, brown cat. Delia never had any fur out of place, ever!

As usual, Delia was washing her fluffy face and her brown, beautifully pointed ears.

'Where have you been?' she gracefully purred. 'Chiko and I have been waiting over an hour for you.' She stopped to lick the inside of her front paw, looked at it, and satisfied that it was spotless, turned her face back to Mischa and continued.

'Only yesterday we decided to meet up in your garden at this time. And not only did you over sleep, you silly Takoda, you completely forgot!'

'I'm sorry, Delia. Honest. I didn't forget. I just fell asleep. Couldn't help it. It was such a lovely dream. Sorry.' Mischa wagged her tail at a very fast pace, keenly hoping that would make up for it.

'Yes I know' chirped Chiko, flying over Mischa's head and landing on the rickety fence. 'Thirty minutes of excessive window tapping seems barely sufficient to wrench you from your dreams! My beak is still sore!'

Mischa pulled a face at Chiko and stuck out her tongue.

'Enough' said Delia, authoritatively raising her paw in the air. 'Today, for the first time ever, I am going to take the two of you to my magic tree. The Tamarix tree. As you will see, this tree, unlike any other in the garden, or indeed anywhere on the planet, flowers all year long. It is a very special tree with magical powers, which I can unleash with my knowledge.

She looked smugly at the surprised pair, who glanced sideways at each other with baffled expressions.

'No one else must know. I do not expect either of you to fall asleep' she added, glaring at Mischa, 'nor be too busy talking to girlfriends' looking down her pink nose at Chiko.

'I will never again oversleep' said Mischa, stifling a yawn.

'Nor me' twittered Chiko, blowing one final kiss to Daisy, his latest in a long stream of girlfriends.

'Good. Then let us embark on our first adventure together' said Delia, raising her paw in a triumphant gesture.

Mischa jumped up and down, excitedly. 'Do you know where we are going? And how long for? And where will we sleep? And what will we eat?'

'All in good time' answered Chiko, shaking his head at Mischa's lack of self-control. 'Delia's magic will take care of everything.' He scratched his short stubby beak against the edge of the fence. 'I hope' he muttered to himself.

Delia delicately walked along the edge of the rickety fence, like a Miss World contestant gliding along a catwalk in front of thousands of people. She leaped through the air and landed on the soft, spongy green grass. The three friends made their way to the corner of the garden where the rickety fence met Mr Clarke's fancy trellis fence. After creeping through the orange and red wallflowers they came across a group of shrubs. The Tamarix, with its splendid, pink, feathery branches, hid quietly under the shade of a large laburnum.

'Never been down here before. It smells funny' whispered Mischa.

'It's a clean, fresh, fragrant smell. You find it different because it doesn't smell of muck and mud' retorted Chiko, ruffling his feathers.

'Shhh' hissed Delia. 'This is a magic tree. Our Tamarix tree. If you have ever observed your garden, Mischa, you wouldn't be surprised to learn that this tree, because it is magical, can flower all year long and flutter magic dust from its feathery flowers. Sit down and copy me.' She crossed her hind legs in the semi-lotus position. When Chiko and Mischa crossed their legs as best as they could, Delia commenced the magic spell:

'Magic. Magic. Around us now,
Take us to our destination.
Make it quick or make it slow,
Lead us through this transformation.'

They disappeared in a thick, orange puff of smoke.

Mischa took her paws away from her eyes and looked around. They were inside a dark, windowless room. It had a strange, damp, musty smell, as though nobody had lived there for several years.

'If this is magic, I'll have a bath every day for a month,' Mischa snorted to herself. 'Where are we?' she moaned. She didn't like the look of the place at all.

'Shhh' hissed Delia again. 'Follow me.'

She led them out of the room and through a dimly lit hall. On the left there were brown doors, and on the right, purple doors. Each door had a handle situated very close to the ground, specially designed for those Takoda belonging to the shorter species. In the distance they could hear a splish–splosh sound. Delia continued down the hallway, with Chiko and Mischa following hot on her trail.

'I want to go home' wailed Mischa.

'Shhh. We're nearly there.'

They arrived at a brown door with the number 2021 on it. Delia opened the door and allowed Mischa to proceed first.

'Aaaahh' squealed Mischa, throwing herself back at the cat.

'Get off of me, Mischa, and behave like a dog!' muttered Delia.

'Isn't that Henry VIII?' enquired Chiko, his head tilted to one side.

'Well done' meowed Delia.

'And didn't he die some time ago' said Mischa, still clutching onto Delia's leg.

'He did' replied Delia. 'This, however, is only a wax figure, created entirely by paw.'

Mischa courageously took a few steps forward and gave Henry VIII a sniff. She walked around him, looking at his odd clothes and the giant ruffle around his neck. She shook her head as she pondered over this strange sight.

'These Human-Bean pets wear the strangest of clothes. And that pink stuff feels so yucky.' Mischa shivered.

'Pink stuff?' said Delia, with an amused look on her pointed face. 'Ah, you mean skin. Human-Being pets need skin, and it doesn't only come in pink, Mischa; it comes in various shades of white, yellow and brown, to the darkest shades of black. Can you imagine what they would look like with our lovely fur or those fluffy feathers?!'

The three of them laughed loudly.

'And they are not Human-Beans, Mischa, they are Human-Beings! You don't plant them in the ground like a runner-bean seed, silly.'

'But, you get French-Beans; they grow in the soil and speak that funny language, just like Madeleine' argued Mischa.

Chiko looked at Delia and smirked.

The sheltie raised her grubby paw and gave Henry VIII a playful shove.

Henry fell backwards with a dull thud and broke into hundreds of pieces.

'Don't do that!' growled Delia, angrily. 'That took weeks to make.'

'Sorry' whimpered Mischa, trying to collect the sadly disfigured wax lumps of Henry VIII into a tidy bundle.

Delia led the way back to the corridor. Chiko flew ahead and into a room where the purple door had been left open.

'Misty Blue' he squealed, excitedly. In the centre of the room stood a very realistic twin of the Scottish singer, Misty Blue. She was dressed in a long blue gown with sequins, and her auburn ringlets framed her face beautifully.

'I love all of her songs' twittered Chiko, and whistled her latest hit, 'Love you, Need you.'

'Practicing for Daisy, are we?' said Delia, sarcastically.

Chiko's red breast extended up to his face as he muttered something obscene under his breath.

'I heard that' Delia retorted. She walked to the back of the room with her bushy tail standing straight in the air. Mischa smothered a giggle and followed Delia, avoiding lumps of dried wax on the floor.

'This' said Delia, in a very authoritative voice, 'is our master. I give you, Cattacitus A. Timmins.'

'Wow' said Mischa, with her mouth wide open. 'Those claws look really long and sharp. Good for chasing birds and vermin.'

Chiko gulped. 'If this were only a wax figure, what would the real thing be like?'

This cat was nearly six feet high and towered over the three friends.

'Cattacitus A. Timmins does not chase birds and mice, you silly dog. He is our leader. He is a master of disguise. He instructs me every day, giving me tasks to perform and nurtures my magical abilities.' She looked up at the huge statue with pride. 'You are both honoured. 'Cattacitus A. Timmins has instructed me to include you in our magic games, in the land of Aurora.'

Chiko and Mischa looked blankly at each other, and then back up to the monstrously large black, wax cat, who bore fierce claws, long sage-like whiskers, piercing orange eyes and a very noble expression on his face.

'Come with me. We will meet the real Cattacitus A. Timmins at a later stage.'

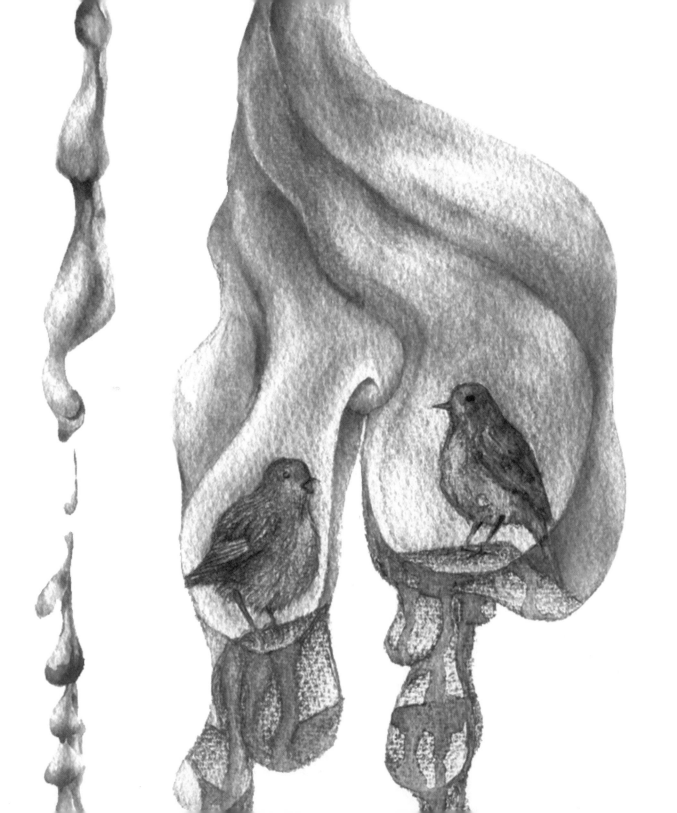

Delia strutted along the long corridor with her tail in the air, and beckoned her two colleagues to follow.' After several dark rooms and various famous wax figures, Mischa yawned.

'Boring' she said to herself.

As they walked along, the splish-splosh sound got louder.

'What's that noise' whispered Chiko to Mischa.

'Dunno. Suppose Delia has another Human-Bean pet for us to look at.'

'Human-Being' corrected Chiko.

Delia stopped in the hall of the third floor and made an announcement.

'Now my friends. I, Delia, the marvellous cat, have a surprise for you.'

She beamed at them from ear to ear as though she had something up her sleeve. Delia led them into a dark grey, gloomy room, cramped with furniture and boxes. The rooms smelled of damp wood and made Mischa feel sick. Delia sat down and slowly curled her long brown tail around her body. She looked around her favourite room, which was even darker than the others; lit only by three, worn down, dirty white candles in brass Human-Being pet shaped holders. Shivers swept through Mischa's body as she walked around the room, sniffing and peering cautiously into boxes, in case Delia's surprise was a dead mouse, or something worse.

'You'll find your surprise in that cupboard,' said Delia, pointing to an ugly green coloured door. 'Your surprise, Chiko, is in that cupboard up there.' She pointed to a grubby, blue coloured door on the wall.

Mischa and Chiko opened their cupboard doors at the same time. At that very moment, the candles flickered, and to Mischa's horror, went out, leaving them in total darkness.

'Eeeeeh' screamed Mischa, as a body fell on top of her. She remained perfectly still and dared not move the body.

'Tee hee' chuckled Chiko, realising what was in his cupboard.

Delia re-lit the candles, restoring the room to its former dimness. Mischa opened her eyes and looked at the body. To her relief, she found herself under a large wax double of herself.

Chiko, being highly amused with his twin, danced around the room clutching the other wax robin tightly.

'These are Doppelgangers. Technically speaking, they're supposed to be your twin ghosts, but these are your wax twins' purred Delia, grandly.

'Doppel what?!' said Mischa, sniffing her twin curiously.

'Doppelganger. Isn't this an exciting moment!'

'Oh' was the only word that could come out of Mischa's mouth, not knowing if this was such a good thing to have. She stood up and felt silly. Having looked and inspected her double all over, Mischa decided that she was quite impressed with the likeness of her double. The colour of the wax fur matched her own shades of brown, gold and white completely. She picked up the wax double and marched around the room, following in Chiko's claw steps.

They had a great time, reeling and dancing around the cluttered room; pulling faces at their doubles; crashing and bumping into chairs and boxes. So much so, that they did not realise that the splish-splosh noise was getting louder.

Suddenly, there was an ear splitting crunch and a very loud howl. Mischa fell, head first, through the floorboards into a large, shallow pot of warm wax.

Delia and Chiko stared through the hole in the floor. Mischa, kicking her legs wildly, turned herself round such that she was completely covered in wax. The pair burst into laughter as Mischa stood up with wax dripping from the whole of her body. Uncovered, were only two little slits, from which her sad, brown eyes stared through, sorrowfully.

'Thanks for your help' she whined.

As Delia and Chiko casually descended to the next floor and into the melting room, they watched Mischa trying to shake the wax from her ears. When she had dried out, Mischa's fur stood on end as stiff as a brush. Her lovely white bib was ruined and looked more like a Roman gladiator's shield.

'Mrs. Jennings is not going to be happy' sobbed Mischa, in tears.

'This is not a problem, my little Takoda. I shall have you looking like a new penny' said Delia, clicking her claws.

Mischa reappeared under the Tamarix tree. She looked up at the rickety fence and saw Delia washing her long brown tail, and in the laburnum tree, Chiko talking to Daisy.

'Mischa! Mischa! Have you bin sleepin' in that muddy corner all afternoon?!' yelled Mrs. Jennings, giving the poor dog a start. Her eyebrows knitted together so closely that Mrs. Jennings now resembled a bulldog.

Mischa barked and ran to her Human-Being pet, giving herself a quick look-down just to make sure that Delia's magic had cleaned her fur thoroughly. Somehow, it had not quite worked, and Mischa's run turned into a slow crawl as she approached Mrs. Jennings, shamefaced. Her tail drooped between her legs as it occurred to her that Mrs. Jennings would now probably think that a bath was in order.

'Oh Mischa. Look at yer fur' said Mrs. Jennings, crossly. 'Have yer no pride in yer appearance. It feels all rough an' stiff as though you've bin sittin' in a cement pit. Oi hope you haven't bin diggin' in me rhubarb patch again.'

'No, no' barked Mischa. 'Why can't you Human-Bean pets understand us like we can understand you?'

'Mmm...' said Mrs. Jennings. 'You have bin up ta somethin.' Yer fur is in very bad shape. Oi'm goin' ta have ta give you a bath, shampoo and probably conditioner.'

'Nooooooooo' howled Mischa, with her long snout in the air.

Mrs. Jennings continued, 'Why can't you be like Mr. Barrowclough's lovely cat, an' keep yourself nice 'n' clean?'

Delia and Chiko giggled, watching on as Mischa was washed with bucket after bucket of water, and doused in pink, bubbly shampoo that smelled of apples.

After her ordeal, Mischa ran around the garden to let her fur dry out completely. She jumped here and there, smiling happily, gathering white daisies in her mouth for Mrs. Jennings.

Suddenly she remembered the wax double of herself, and could not remember whether she had seen or dreamt it!

'Eeeeeeh' screamed Mischa, once more, thinking that she was imagining things. She scattered her daisies over the lawn and ran in circles with her tail between her legs.

'Tee hee' chuckled Chiko. 'Have another dance, another fall, another shampoo and conditioner. Do you think Mrs. Jennings could manage to put your fur in rollers? I think a ringlet style would suit you far better than that shaggy look!'

'Huh!' said Mischa, grumpily. 'This means double trouble!'

Chapter 2: Mischa's Birthday

'Mischa. Mischa! Wake up!' called Mrs. Jennings, on the last day of March. 'It's yer birthday! Get up you lazy girl! Come 'n' see what Oi've got hidden inside this parcel.' Mrs. Jennings paced around the living room with so much energy that her pink slippers were in danger of wearing a patch in the carpet. Mischa yawned noisily. She looked up at Mrs. Jennings' beaming face with a puzzled look through big, brown eyes. Suddenly, as if someone had just switched on the light, it dawned on Mischa that it was her birthday, and she jumped up, laughing and barking at the same time

'It's my birthday! It's my birthday! I'm four. I'm four today.' She skipped, hopped, jumped and finally chased her tail round and round and round.

'All right, Mischa, calm down. Let's open yer present.' Mrs. Jennings slowly unwrapped the small silver parcel with a huge, red bow on the top. Inside, was a beautiful red collar with an heart-shaped golden tag. On it, in bold capitals, it read:

MISCHA JENNINGS
BRACKEN BARN
MIDSOMER-ATTE-STOKE
SOMERSET

Harriet Jennings tied the collar around Mischa's neck. It suited her perfectly. Mischa jumped onto Mrs. Jennings' lap and smothered her in kisses. Wagging her tail at a tremendous pace she panted, 'Thank you so much, Mrs. J., I love it!' and barked delightedly. 'Good girl' said Mrs. Jennings, gently stroking the sheltie's soft fur. She walked into the kitchen and took two tins of dog food from the pine cupboard. 'Look! Oi've got two tins of Bowzers. Chicken, ham and gravy; or pork, stuffing and gravy. Which one do yer want?' Mrs. Jennings held out the two tins.

Mischa jumped up and down excitedly and bounced her nose off the pork, stuffing and gravy tin.

'Pork! Pork!' she woofed, eagerly. Mrs. Jennings gave Mischa a bowl of Bowzers, which she scoffed down in no time at all.

'My! What a big appetite yer've got fer such a small dog. Oi think it's time for your run around the garden. When yer come back inside Oi'll have a lovely birthday tea ready for yer.'

Mischa waited by the backdoor. After a good, tasty meal, there was nothing better than an energetic run around the garden, a chase with Chiko and Daisy, and to have her daily chat with Delia. Mrs. Jennings waddled over to Mischa and unlocked the stiff, creaking door, exposing her to the mad, gusty winds of March.

'Off yer go. But don't be too long 'cos Mac is comin' round to see yer this afternoon.' Mischa, who had already bounded half way down the garden, stopped dead in her tracks.

'Mac? Oh no! I'll do anything to get out of seeing that awful West Highland Terrier. He gives me such a headache with that yipping and yelping in that awful Scottish accent. Crumbs, he's just like his Human-Bean pet, Heather Mac B. She never stops talking, either. All that "wee" and "lassie" rubbish. And don't even get me started on their funny skirts. Even Hamish Mac B. wears one! It's unbelievable, an Alpha Human-Bean in a skirt!' She sat down and scratched her belly. 'Huh! It's so annoying! I don't know why I have to spend my birthday speaking to that whippersnapper, greedy, talk-all-the-time dog. All he ever wants to do is yak and chew bones, day and night.' She gave a big sigh and pulled a face. 'C'est la vie.'

Mischa ran to the bottom of the garden and found Delia and Chiko balanced on the rickety fence, which rocked backwards and forwards. Even though it was very windy, both the cat and the bird balanced precariously on the fence, as though it was a swing. Just to make a change, Delia was washing her pretty brown face and long white whiskers.

'It's my birthday! I'm four, I'm four today!' barked Mischa, excitedly.

'Did you remember?' knowing that they always gave her a card and a bone for her birthday. Delia and Chiko looked at each other and shrugged their shoulders.

'Sorry, Mischa, we forgot' mumbled Chiko, apologetically, skipping along the fence. Mischa looked from Chiko to Delia, then down to her front paws. She looked a sorry sight. Her head hung low and a single tear fell from her eye.

'Never mind' continued Chiko, darting his head this way and that. 'Let's see where Delia's magic will take us today.' The robin swiftly flew off to the feathery Tamarix tree, and perched on a large branch adorned with pink fluffy flowers.

'Stupid magic. Nobody remembered my birthday. Pfft.' thought Mischa, grumpily. Delia, sensing that the sheltie was going to be awkward, jumped down beside Mischa and licked her nose.

'Ugh' said Mischa, wiping her nose with her paw.

'Race you' shouted the cat.

Mischa and Delia scrambled through the shrubs and collapsed under the Tamarix in giggles. They crossed their legs, held each other's paws and wings, and waited for Delia's magic.

'Magic. Magic. From my powers,
Take us to a place full of flowers....'

'Flowers? Huh' said Mischa, rudely. 'I don't want to see flowers on my birthday.'

'Shhhh' hissed the cat.

'Guide us through these cold winds swiftly,
And relieve us of Mischa's terrible misery.'

The three friends disappeared in a cloud of white smoke, only to reappear in an enchanted forest. The trees and grass were various shades of bright green, and wafted peppermint and spearmint odours into the air.

Pop-pop, pop, pop!

Flowers began to spring up everywhere. Flowers of every shade, colour and size, and of such beauty, that Mischa gasped in amazement. She was so overcome with the beauty of the flowers that she could not imagine a more wonderful place on earth. She lifted her long nose and inhaled the wonderful scents that drifted around her.

'Sweets!' she cried.

'I beg you pardon' said Delia, lazily lapping her paw, which she had just dipped into a nearby pond of creamy, white chocolate milk.

'The flowers are made of sweets!' exclaimed Mischa. 'I can smell jelly babies, liquorice, lemon toffee bonbons, cola drops, toffees, pear drops, strawberry sherbet, chocolate eclairs, humbugs - oh look! - flying Saucers!' and before they knew it, Mischa gobbled up paw-fulls of flowers.

'Come over here, Delia. Look what I've found' whistled Chiko. 'Come and see this magnificent cottage.' He spotted Mischa greedily devouring the flowers.

'Mischa! Mischa! Stop eating those flowers. You'll be sick!' he shouted, jumping from twig to twig. 'Mischa, stop that at once. Stop I say!', screeching at the very top of his voice.

Mischa managed to swallow another pink marshmallow flower, and reluctantly followed Delia into the front garden of the bright yellow cottage.

'What is this place?' asked Mischa, looking up inquisitively at the enormous cola bottle shaped chimney.

'It's a magic cottage' answered Delia, authoritatively.

Mischa and Delia walked up the raspberry drop encrusted path, which led round to the back garden.

'Isn't this marvellous?' said Mischa, dreamily. 'I wish I could live here, surrounded by sweets and chocolates all day long. My very own never ending supply of goodies.'

Delia and Chiko looked at each other and laughed.

As they entered the back garden, Mischa saw a huge table decorated with a bright red and white checked tablecloth. Then, bright red cups, saucers and spoons appeared out of the air and arranged themselves neatly on the table. Flying through the air came a triple layered, chocolate flavoured cream cake, filled with mashed bananas, and settled in the middle. It was baked in the shape of a large bone, and on it, "Mischa" had been written in pink icing. As a finishing touch, an orange and brown iced figure of a Shetland sheepdog was placed in the centre.

Mischa sat down with an astonished look on her face.

Ten beautiful faeries, with bright golden hair and dressed in silver gowns, descended down around the friends and sat upon orange flavoured toadstools dotted with red jellies. The faeries produced ten golden harps, and begun to pluck the most angelic music.

Cascades of twinkling quavers and semi-quavers were showered upon the guests as they listened intently to the shimmering sounds. Small and large animals and birds came out of their hiding places and sang "Happy Birthday" to Mischa, and danced around her in a big circle. Mischa listed on to the wonderful sounds, ranging from the high chirping tweets from the robins, swallows and sparrows, to the low boyish yawls of the foxes, minks, badgers and hedgehogs.

The little sheltie sat down with tears in her eyes. Mischa felt so ungrateful for thinking the worst of Chiko and Delia for not sending her a card. She had even contemplated not sending them a card for their birthdays; but instead of forgetting her birthday, they had arranged a wonderful surprise party. How silly she had been!

After "Happy Birthday" had been sung, the animals, birds and faeries took their places around the table, with Mischa and Delia seated at the ends.

Chiko and his fellow birds were strategically placed on mini mock orange trees on the table, so that they could see all that was going on, and be first to nibble on what ever cakes they liked!

Delia clicked her front right claws together and said 'Delicious foods'.

Instantly, star shaped pineapple and strawberry flavoured jellies, toffee filled chocolates, bowls upon bowls of assorted sweets, and mini bone-shaped sandwiches, appeared from thin air and spread themselves over the table. Jugs of purple grape, melon and honey juice, and pink rose-flavoured cordial, flew down and filled the empty crystal goblets.

The guests put on their shiny red party hats, and placed matching red napkins on their laps.

The partygoers gorged themselves silly, especially Mischa!

Having eaten plates of banana filled birthday cake, raspberry jelly, white chocolate drops, blackcurrant wine gums and several pink and white marshmallows, the greedy dog stood up and clutched her belly.

'Ooooooh' she groaned, loudly, 'I wish I hadn't eaten so much.'

'Told you so' cheeked the robin, making 'tut tut' noises to himself.

'Why don't you have another plate of jelly babies? May be I could interest you in devouring the whole cottage?' suggested a small lamb.

Mischa snarled angrily at the lamb, and bore her little white teeth from her slightly upturned top lip.

Delia finished off her sardine sandwich and cleaned her mouth and long whiskers, thoroughly. She looked at Mischa and shook her head.

'Come on, it's time to go home' she purred, feeling that things were starting to get a little out of hand.

The animals, birds and faeries thanked Delia and her friends for coming. They sang "Happy Birthday" once more for Mischa, who blushed from ear to ear.

'That was lovely' said Mischa, still grinning. 'Oh dear! I forgot Mac is coming for tea, or should I say he's been and gone? What a pity if I've missed that annoying little dog' she giggled, naughtily.

'Let's hurry, I'll have the last laugh if he is still waiting for you' twittered Chiko. 'Mind you, I suspect he has already eaten you out of house and bone.'

Mischa reappeared under the feathery Tamarix. She looked up at the rickety fence and found Delia and Chiko balanced precariously on the narrow edge, still blowing from side to side in the wind. She turned towards the house and saw Mrs. Jennings standing outside with her hands on her hips. She opened her eyes widely and thought, 'here comes trouble!'

'Mischa! Where have yer been?' barked Mrs. Jennings crossly. Mischa even thought that Mrs. Jennings' bark was louder and deeper than Sorcha's, the Irish wolfhound.

Mischa ran over to her and wagged her tail.

'Mischa, Mac has been waiting over ten minutes for you. Oi've called you over an' over again. If Oi've told yer once, Oi've told yer a hundred times, don't keep yer company waitin!' Oi don't know why you spend so much time milling around the end of the garden where there's nothin' but trees, bushes and slimy mud. Oi suppose you fell asleep again, under one of tho' old shrubs. Well, t'is yer birthday.' She took a deep breath and, in a much softer tone, continued, 'as you are here we can start your birthday tea. Oi made you a huge, green birthday cake, with a mixture of marshmallow and banana filling. And Mac has brought over six, extra large crunch biscuit bones. Aren't you a lucky girl?'

Mac stuck his head out from behind Mrs. Jennings' chunky legs and yelped in his very high pitched Scottish accent, 'Mischa, ma bonnie lassie. Happy Birthday to ye. Let's discuss our news over a wee slice of cake an' bones. Err, perhaps Mrs. Jennings could oblige me with a wee pokey hat and a wee dram as well?'

Mrs. Jennings placed a dish of water on the floor for Mac. 'Here you go my luvely. Have a nice drink o' water.'

Mac sniffed it, stuck his nose in the air and said to Mischa 'Och! Why cannae

Mrs. J. understand that I said a wee dram, not this Adam's ale? I'm droothy!' He shook his head, scratched his belly and took a bone instead.

After another hour of eating, Mischa looked out of the French windows at Chiko and Delia, with a fat, bloated, green tinted face, and an equally full belly.

Delia and Chiko looked at each other and quaked with laughter. In fact, Chiko reeled around so much that he fell off the oak bench on which he was sitting.

'Because you were so greedy, announced Delia, haughtily, 'you'll have to let Mac have all of his bones and eat them!'

Chapter 3: The Magic Pumpkins

The following morning, Mischa woke with a dreadful pain in her belly.

'Yowhooooooo! Yowhooooooooo!' she moaned, pitifully.

Mrs. Jennings rolled down the stairs as fast as she could, calling 'Mischa, Mischa? What is it? What's wrong? Are yer sick? Have yer hurt yer paws? Is yer collar too tight?'

Mischa remained still, in her bed, with her white tipped paws stretched flat in front, with her long brown nose leaning heavily on them.

'Yowhooo' she cried, once more, burying her nose deeper into her paws.

'Goodness!' exclaimed Mrs. Jennings. 'Yer must ha' bin sick yesterday an' Oi didn' even realise. No wonder yer didn' want anymore green birthday cake last night. Oi hope yer not comin' down with the same illness as tha' St. Bernard from down th' road.'

Suddenly Mischa felt very queasy, not least after the word *green* was mentioned. She got out of bed and walked to the backdoor. With her tummy wobbling and making funny noises, she whined to go out.

'If yer not better by the time yer get back, Oi'll ha' to take yer to see Doctor Sortuite,' warned Mrs. Jennings.

'No! No! I won't go!' barked Mischa, loudly, with her tail between her legs.

'I won't see that incompetent Human-Bean today, or any other day. In fact, the last time I saw that Bean, who, by the way, thinks he knows everything about Takoda, I couldn't walk properly for a whole week. That Bean is a fool! He doesn't know the first thing about gold fish, let alone dogs.'

Mischa stomped off down the garden.

Mrs. Jennings nodded wisely as though she had understood every word, waved good-bye and closed the backdoor with a bang.

'Huh!' said Mischa, rudely. 'Human-Bean pets.'

Mischa continued the rest of the journey to the rickety fence by hopping along on three legs, while she clutched her belly with her remaining paw.

'Help me, please' wailed Mischa, with her mouth barely moving.

'Uno momento, ventriloquist' interrupted the cheeky robin, in a mock Italian accent that he had picked up from Dino, the Italian duck. He gave Delia two final sweeps with a pink coral comb, which he clutched with his spindly little claws, then sat down and stared at Mischa with his head tilted to one side.

Delia turned around and looked at Mischa, without even as much as one strand of hair out of place, and looking more stunning than ever.

'What's the matter, my poor little dog' she purred, smugly. 'Have you got tummy ache?'

Mischa looked up with her sad brown eyes. 'Well yes' admitted Mischa, 'How did you know?'

'Cats are remarkably purrfectly creatures. We have the most marvellous sense of deduction. Besides, I don't have to think like Einstein to know that after eating all of those cakes and flowers, yesterday, you were bound to have a bellyache. You see, Mischa, it's only a matter of time.'

'Thank you for your lecture, you're quite right. Now will you help me, please?'

All right. What can I do for you?' smiled Delia, delighted that she seemed superior to Mischa.

'Give her a six foot sun flower to munch,' suggested Chiko, casually tucking a red breast feather into place.

Mischa growled angrily.

'Chiko, please! We will help Mischa, not make her feel worse.'

'Okay, okay. I'll keep my thoughts and opinions to myself from now on. In fact, I will never give my opinion on anything, ever again' said Chiko, grumpily.

'Hooray for that' muttered Mischa to herself.

'What was that?' snorted Chiko.

'I said, "What a nice cat"' answered Mischa, through her teeth. 'Now, where was I? Ah yes, if I am not better by the time I get back home, Mrs. Jennings will take me to see Doctor Sort U. Out.'

'Serves you right for being such a pig!' mumbled Chiko.

'Wait, Chiko. Isn't that the Human-Being pet who thinks he's Doctor Doolittle? Hmmm, you do have a problem. I wouldn't trust that pet for all the mice of China' said Delia, ignoring Chiko's little out burst.

Mischa's head dropped heavily in the most melancholy manner.

'Come with us to the magic tree. I'm sure that there will be a cure for you there. I didn't mean to be so unkind. I know what it's like to see Doctor Sort U. Out' said Delia, leading the way. 'The last time Mr. Barrowclough brought me into the surgery, he opened my mouth so wide that I was almost tempted to bite him.'

As they walked towards the Tamarix, Delia suddenly stopped and turned around.

'Wait, where's Chiko?'

Mischa, who was still feeling very sorry for herself, shook her head slowly. Delia scoured the garden with her sharp eyes but still could not locate the robin. Chiko had indeed vanished.

'Chiko, Chiko, it's time to go' meowed Delia.

A muffled whistling came from the direction of a conifer, near the laburnum tree. Delia and Mischa investigated, and much to their disgust, found Chiko with his head buried inside an extra large slice of Mischa's birthday cake. Mrs. Jennings had placed some outside for the birds, that morning.

'Mischa won't be the only one with tummy ache, today' grumbled Delia, to herself.

The two of them eventually managed to wrestle Chiko away from the slice of cake, but even then, his beak was filled to capacity with the green sponge.

'Magic. Magic. Where'er you are,
Eliminate all illness now.
Take the memories of those cakes,
And rid Mischa of her belly ache.'

They disappeared in a thick green mist and were transported to a land far away. After the mist had cleared, Mischa and Chiko found that they were sitting in a large field, filled with at least five hundred pumpkins of every shape and size.

It was a magic pumpkin field! Each pumpkin had a bright orange face with large, friendly green eyes, and a wide toothless mouth. They smiled and wobbled from side to side, scraping and bowing at Delia as best as they could.

'Magic pumpkins, please make yourselves comfortable' roared Delia, so that even the pumpkins at the back of the field could hear. 'Today we have to give some very serious consideration to Mischa's tummy ache' she placed one brown paw on Mischa's shoulder.

Chiko whispered something into a baby pumpkin's ear. Within seconds, titters emerged from the back of the field. Several rumours spread rapidly from one pumpkin to the next, until there was complete uproar.

'Bellyache?' said the baby pumpkin.

'No wonder, after eating all those cakes and sweets.'

'And chocolates' added an enormous pumpkin with wrinkled skin.

'What about the flowers? Fancy eating flowers! That's asking for trouble' said a lady pumpkin, with long green hair.

'Flowers. Haho!' laughed the magic pumpkins.

Mischa was not amused. The pumpkins carried on wobbling with laughter. Chiko and Delia joined in and could not stop.

'Stop it, stop it, stop it!' raged Mischa, glowering at everyone.

Delia stood up and raised her paw in the air.

'Silence please, Chiko, Magic Pumpkins' said Delia, loudly. 'This is no longer a laughing matter. Today, we are here to help our colleague', she gazed around the field looking at the round orange faces, 'who happens to be very, very, sick. And' she nodded authoritatively, whilst drawing a deep breath, 'will feel far worse if she has to see her vet, Doctor Sort U. Out.'

The silence lasted for a brief thirty seconds, when muffled giggling started

up at the back of the field, led by an extraordinarily large pumpkin with a gruff voice.

'Mischa - silence please pumpkins, and Chiko - to relieve yourself of your pain, you must perform an act, trick or dance, perhaps even sing, to each and every pumpkin in this field.' She nodded to Mischa and smiled to the pumpkins.

'Wha, wha, what? Ehh ?' cried Mischa, hardly able to believe her own ears. 'There are hundreds of pumpkins in this field.'

'Hmm, yes I know' said Delia, trying very hard to hide a snigger.

Chiko was in stitches. He placed his wings over his beak in an attempt to control his laughter; but the harder he tried, the more he wanted to laugh. Eventually, he caved in and just rolled over and over in the grass in hoots of laughter and giggles. The Magic Pumpkins followed suit because it did not take much to make them laugh.

'Hurry up, Mischa' they cried out, together, 'We can't wait all day.'

There were shouts of encouragement, squeals of delight and guffaws, mixed in with wobbling pumpkin heads and stalks, rolling around in the grass.

'No, no, no' barked Mischa, furiously.

'Oh, very well. I guess you want to see Doctor Sort U. Out' said Delia.

Mischa gave in, reluctantly, and began her performance.

She balanced on her front paws, juggled five balls, and sang two verses of "How much is that doggy in the window", followed by a cartwheel, a double somersault, and a mime of a drunken dog walking down the street.

She was half way through her break-dance routine, which she copied from Mrs. Jennings' talking, square box on legs, when she realised that everyone had erupted in laughter. The Magic Pumpkins, Chiko and Delia laughed so much that tears rolled down their faces. There were stalks, wings and paws in the air as they threw themselves around the grass and curled in hysteria.

'How dare you laugh at me' fumed Mischa, baring her teeth viciously. She put her paws on her hips and stared at them.

'Mischa, calm down, tee-hee,' they spluttered together.

'Calm down? Calm down? Are you all mad?!' barked Mischa.

'We've never seen a dog perform a break-dance routine before,' cried Chiko. 'You were so funny, you should've seen yourself. Will you do it again? Pretty please? Perhaps in slow motion ? Please, Mischa!'

'No, no, no!' barked the sheltie, angrily. She turned away from the pumpkins, Delia and Chiko, and stomped off.

'April Fools Day!' they sang out, together.

Mischa turned around, red-faced, with a shocked expression on her little pointed face. She was absolutely horrified that she could have fallen for such a silly trick.

'Why me?' she panted at the field of laughing pumpkins. 'Why me' she grumbled to Delia.

The others laughed so much that they could not even hear a word of what Mischa was saying. The pumpkins hopped over the field, bouncing on their heads, pulling faces at each other and giving loud whoops and cheers. Delia caterwauled so loudly, and in such an unladylike fashion, that even Mischa had to see the funny side of things.

She lay down in the sweet scented grass, rolled onto her back and churned her paws in the air, laughing and giggling.

After everyone had settled down, and the last tears wiped away, Mischa stood up and said, 'What about my tummy ache?'

'It's gone' replied Delia.

'So it has!' said a euphoric Mischa, 'And I didn't even notice!'

'It's amazing what laughter can do for you' said the cat, wisely.

'Mission accomplished!' cheered Chiko.

Mrs. Jennings opened the back door, squinted her grey eyes and peered across the garden. The golden brown sheltie ran the length of the garden and up to her Human-Being pet.

'Shall Oi take you to Doctor Sortuite?' enquired Mrs. Jennings, with a puzzled look on her face.

'No!' barked Mischa, rolling over twice and then jumping up and down with conviction.

'Well, suppose there's no need fer you ta see the vet today. Still can't believe yer feelin' better; eh, never mind. You've certainly perked up this afternoon. Maybe yer had a nice long nap. Whatever happened to yer, why, it's just like magic.'

'Yes! Yes!' barked Mischa. 'Magic! Magic! Thank Delia for magic cos now I don't have to see that stupid Human-Bean.'

'Now, because yer've made such a good recovery, yer must be starving' said Mrs. Jennings, with her hands on her extremely large, round hips.

'Yes! Yes! Food! Banana cake!' squealed Mischa, delightedly, standing on her hind legs and waving her front paws.

'It just so happens that Oi've come from the supermarket. And yer wouldn't believe the special offer they had ta-day: pumpkins! An' Oi know how much yer like pie. So Oi'm goin' ta make you the largest, yummiest pumpkin-pie yer've ever laid eyes on!'

Mischa stood still and stared at Mrs. Jennings with her mouth wide open in disbelief.

'Oi thought you'd be speechless.' She gave the sheltie a pat on the head and went inside.

Chapter 4: The Visitor

Early next morning, a letter fell onto the mat by the front door with a dull thud. As always, mail was accompanied with a free copy of the *Midsomer-Atte-Stoke Gazette*. Mrs. Jennings wobbled out of the kitchen and when picking up the letter, smiled broadly.

Good. It's from my sister, Jemimah. Now, where did Oi leave my glasses? Oi think Oi left them on the coffee table.'

Mischa ran back to the living room and gingerly picked up with her mouth the brown case containing Mrs. Jennings' glasses. She brought them back to the kitchen where Mrs. Jennings had just poured herself a fresh cup of tea. Mrs. Jennings also gave Mischa a small bowl of warm tea and a custard cream biscuit.

'Thank you, Mischa. How did ya know Oi needed these?' She stroked the sheltie's face gently.

'Cos I can understand Human-Bean pet language, silly' woofed Mischa, smiling up at Mrs. Jennings.

Harriet Jennings opened the white envelope and pulled out the enclosed sheet of pink paper with very neat writing. She then placed her brown bifocal glasses on her nose and studied the letter.

Mischa, meanwhile, trotted back to the front door and gave two sharp barks.

'It's no use,' said Mrs. Jennings, with a sigh, the postman will be down the next street by now. Really, yer gettin' very lazy these days. When ya were a puppy you scared the postman stiff. Now Oi'm sure tha' you'd welcome burglars with open paws.'

'Of course I wouldn't,' growled an angry Mischa, her pride badly hurt. 'I just can't be bothered.'

After reading the letter, Mrs. Jennings clapped her hands and beamed with excitement. 'Marnie-Rae is coming to visit us! Let me see now, today's the second - mmmm - she will be arriving at the railway station a' noon the day after tomorra.

Oh Oi do so love Marnie-Rae, she's such a good girl. So well mannered, cheerful, bright; long, shiny golden hair, always clean and tidy, not like Matthew. Don't know how a brother and sister can be so different. She bein' so good an' all. She's such a lovely ten year old, Oi wish she were mine.' Mrs. Jennings stared into space, dreaming of what could have been.

Mischa jumped up and down with joy and barked happily. She, too, loved Marnie-Rae for her hugs and cuddles and very gentle manners. She always did the right thing and was never rude, unlike Matthew.

Mischa rolled onto her back and exercised her paws by churning them in a cycling motion, for she knew that she would have to be fit for the three mile walk down to the Country Park. 'Mmmmm, and Marnie-Rae always brings me a bone. That's something else to look forward to.' Mischa smiled with glee.

Mrs. Jennings stood up to refill the worn black kettle, for yet another cup of tea, when the doorbell rang.

'Who's there? Who's there?!' barked Mischa, noisily, trying to prove that she was still able to scare off burglars.

'Good girl, well done. Now, let's see who's at the door.' Mischa, still excited, poised herself at the front door. 'Get down! How am Oi suppose to open the door when yer jumpin' up an' down in front of me?'

Mrs. Jennings slowly opened the door, with Mischa's head also peering out, from between her fat knees and under her yellow daisy apron. Mischa's eyes fell upon the familiar black hobnailed boots, up the tattered blue jeans, the navy army style jersey, and those small, brown, piggy eyes of Matthew Orrible, Marnie-Rae's big brother. Mischa yelped in surprise and ran to her usual hiding place, behind the sofa.

'Matthew, how are ya?' cooed Mrs. Jennings, like a frightened pigeon.

''Allo Auntie 'Arriet. How's it goin'?' grunted Matthew, in his finest Cockney accent.

'Oi'm fine. How's yer family? Oi thought Marnie-Rae was coming to stay. Is she still travelling down ta' Midsomer-Atte-Stoke?'

'She was, only now she's caught a cold, an' can't come. Me mum an' dad are okay and send their luv. By the way, I fowt I'd come an' see you an the fluffy dog for a few days, that is if you don't mind?' said Matthew, smiling as angelically as he could. 'Me mum did try ringin' you, but your phone must broken or off the hook.'

'Of course Oi don't mind ya stayin'. Make yerself at home. You know where everything is' said Mrs. Jennings, forcing herself to smile so much that the lines around her nose seemed to form whiskers.

'Me mum fought I could give you a hand around the house an' in the garden. Or play wif your luvely dog', beaming his broadest fake smile.

Mischa's heart dropped with disappointment. 'A few days? You needn't have bothered coming at all' muttered Mischa, gloomily from behind the sofa. 'I was so looking forward to seeing Marnie-Rae, having the house filled with the scent of lemons and lavender, and now this awful boy is here instead. Good grief! Dogs have the most awful bad luck. Oh what shall I do? Where can I hide? And when will he go?'

'Mischa! Mischa! Where are you?' called Mrs. Jennings, loudly. 'Come an' see Matthew. Don't go hiding an' being rude.'

'Oh dear, why must she put me through this ordeal?' Mischa crept out from behind the sofa and slunk into the kitchen, eyeing Matthew's boots, ominously.

'Go on, he won't bite you. Give Matthew your paw' prompted Mrs. Jennings, taking Matthew's bag up to the spare room.

'I wouldn't put it past him' growled Mischa, sarcastically. She tiptoed closer to Matthew and sat down in front of him with her ears pressed flat against her head, to show her dislike.

'Mischa ol' gal. It's bin a long time, aint it?' Matthew's voice grated like an old washing machine on its last legs, and he proceeded to ratchet poor Mischa's paw up and down as though it was a lever.

'Not long enough' whined the sheltie.

Mischa banged her tail against the carpet and turned to creep back into the living room.

Matthew picked up the local gazette and grinned broadly.

'Hey, Auntie 'Arriet' he bellowed, as Mrs. Jennings made her way back down the stairs. 'Did ya see the headlines in the Gazette? You've got some weird, wild cat prowling around in this part of the county.'

'Wild cat ehh?' repeated Mrs. Jennings, scratching her head.

'Yep. Says here "It's been spotted by six people so far, in different locations around Somerset." It's some kinda large wild kitty wif a mean streak that has injured, taken other animals, and has even killed two sheep. It says, "If seen, do not approach this highly dangerous creature. Contact the police immediately."' Matthew brandished his catapult, lovingly, 'unless I get to it first', and laughed, wickedly.

'Oi wonder if it's some kind a' panther tha' has escaped from a circus' said Mrs. Jennings, cringing up her nose. 'We had a kangaroo skip the circus two years ago. They found him in a field of barley, havin' a great time.' She scratched her nose. 'What do you think abou' tha', Mischa? Wild cats, eh?' She shook her head and went to fill the battered, cast iron kettle, forgetting that she had only filled it a few minutes earlier.

Mischa put her snout in the air and snorted 'Cats! Pfft! The only danger they pose is that stinky alley-cat smell.' She turned and walked over to the French windows to see if Chiko was in the garden.

'Yowhoo!' cried Mischa, as a rubber band, fired by Matthew and his catapult, hit her sharply on her bottom. She ran back into the kitchen and past Mrs. Jennings and scratched wildly at the back door to get out.

'Keep yer fur on' said Mrs. Jennings. 'Sometimes Oi don't know what goes on inside that little head of yours. You can go out and play for a while, but Oi'll leave the door open so you can come back and get Matthew. Oi'm sure he'll join you for a nice walk after he's had a slice of my cream cake and a cup of tea.'

'Huh' groaned Mischa, 'that's all I need.'

Mischa ran as fast as she could towards the rickety fence, and hid beneath a scantily clad rose bush, just in case Matthew was watching from the French windows. Mischa looked up at Delia and Chiko with terror in her eyes. She quaked with fear and laid her ears flat against her head.

'I know! Don't tell me...' meowed Delia. 'Your symptoms tell me that Matthew Orrible is inside your house at this very minute.'

Mischa nodded her head, sorrowfully. 'It's terrible, he's got that contraption that fires objects and he hit me on my...', and turned to look at her rump. 'Marnie-Rae was supposed to come and stay, but she's sick. Now we've got this evil boy instead.'

'Well, we could entertain him with some magic from the Tamarix, before he gets out of hand' said Delia, ruefully pointing her perfectly manicured nail to her pink nose.

'Now that's a brilliant idea' chirped Chiko, delightedly, remembering all too well, Matthew's last visit.

Chiko flew behind Delia and Mischa as they headed to the house. Though armed with a small branch from the Tamarix, they knew to expect tricks from Matthew. Indeed, the last time they had met, the pesky boy had fired his catapult at Chiko, knocking him off his garden perch.

'Come on, hurry up!' twittered Chiko, nervously, 'Mrs. J. is upstairs. I've just seen her face peering out of the window.'

The three friends tiptoed through the backdoor and found Matthew sitting on the sofa in the living room.

Delia ran quickly towards Matthew and shook the Tamarix branch in his face, dusting him in a fine powder.

Matthew fell into a deep sleep, and as he slept, he dreamed the strangest dream. He watched everything unfold as though it were in slow motion. The Takoda assumed the semi-lotus position, and Delia recited her magic spell.

'Magic in our darkest hour,
Take us far from Matthew's grasp,
Carry us swiftly to your caverns,
Guarded by your grizzly bear, Bowyer.'

They smiled cheekily at Matthew.

Mrs. Jennings living room was instantly transformed. The three friends now found themselves in a vast snow-covered land.

A blanket of white stretched towards the horizon. The realm consisted of snow covered trees, ice, more snow, and an accompanying bitterly cold wind. The weak rays of sun could barely pierce the dark, fat clouds that threatened another bout of snow. It looked like an ominous scene from a horror movie.

'Where are we?' quivered Mischa, huddling herself into a ball to keep warm. As if to save her from insanity, she heard a deep bark. It came from Willow, a malamute who came forward to greet her guests. 'Welcome to Alaska!'

'It's beautiful' said Delia, admiring a snow wolf walking through the snow trimmed trees, blending in, white upon white, in the vast expanse of snow and ice. Chiko, meanwhile, shivered nearby, his little wings wobbling in the freezing conditions.

'Is it always this cold?' said Mischa, with chattering teeth.

'Yes, for most of the year' nodded Willow, nobly, 'that's why we Malamutes have thick, warm coats. Follow me please.'

Delia, Mischa and Willow trudged across the snow - their paws sinking deeply into the soft cold powder. Chiko, however, partially buried himself inside Willow's coat in an attempt to keep warm.

'Cor blimey!' said Matthew, as he watched the malamute, the robin, the sheltie and the cat disappear into a small black hole under the branches of a snow-covered black spruce.

'Those pesky creatures 'ave brought me to this weird frozen place. I'm following with me catapult.' He traced the paw steps through the snowfields, to the black spruce, and into a very, very dark cave. It was a very narrow cave with a low roof. Menacing stalactites dripped icy water. Shivering with cold, Matthew was glad he wore a thick vest.

Matthew, crouching to avoid the icicles, paused every so often to listen for sounds. Further down the passageway, the familiar sound of barking dogs finally

reached his ears. He staggered slowly towards the sounds, cautiously feeling his way along the cave wall. A pat to his back pocket confirmed the presence of the catapult.

The narrow passageway opened up into a massive cavern, illuminated by thousands upon thousands of colourful, brightly lit faerie lights, housed inside icicles which dangled from the ceiling. The walls glistened as though specks of silver and gold were embedded in them. It was an amazing sight, and Matthew could only rub his eyes in disbelief.

In the middle of the cavern was a crystal clear lake, home to scores of rainbow-striped fish who darted throughout. Turning towards the walls, Matthew was next astonished to see hundreds of tiny men: Elves! Alaskan Elves! The Elves wore green suits and little green safety helmets. Each man busily picked away at the cavern walls with a tiny axe. They each seemed to be sculpturing their very own design into the face of the wall, and as they worked they sang a song:

'With my axe I pick this ice,
Each little tap makes a face that's nice,
Every time I hit this wall,
I make my sculpture tall.'

'Look! He's followed us!' said Mischa, as she caught sight of Matthew in the distance. 'He's here!'

'Ha ha!' laughed Matthew, crudely. 'You fought you could fool me dog; well lemme tell you somefing, I ain't as daft as I look...you know wat I mean?' He brandished his catapult, once again, threateningly.

'Who are you kidding?' barked Mischa.

'There's more brains in a carrot than in your head' added Chiko.

Matthew raised his catapult with his dirty hands and waved it with intimidation at Mischa. He bent over to find some pieces of ice, and fired them at the poor dog.

'Ouch!' screamed Mischa, with an ear-piercing howl.

'You'll be so sorry you followed us here', whispered a malevolent Delia, smiling cynically.

'Grizzly Bear,
If you're here,
Come and sort out this bullyboy.
Teach him a lesson,
Make it quick,
Then we'll laugh at him
'Til he's sick.'

Matthew stared angrily at his victims and laughed rudely. 'What a load of tripe! What screechy kind of song was that? You can't frighten me - you're nothin' but dumb animals! I'll pin you by yer tails and stamp on ya with me heavy boots. And you', laughing at Willow, 'ain't even got two eyes that are the same colour! Ha ha, one blue and one brown. Freak! Freak! And as for you Mischa, you think everybody luves you, but they don't! You're a stupid short dog that looks like a chopped down version of Lassie! And yer can't even catch a ball! An as fer me cute sister, I made Marnie-Rae stay home wif a cold! I poured a buckit of water over 'er head! Ha ha, you flea ridden mutt, I'll give you what for. Dumb animals!'

Matthew gave a bloodcurdling laugh and charged towards Willow and Mischa, hurling aside any elves that stood in his way. He whooped a horrendous war cry as he gave the poor sheltie the most enormous kick with this hobnailed boot. Mischa tumbled many times until she crashed into the cavern wall, sending shards of ice flying in all directions.

Mischa lay sore, dazed on the cave floor. Willow raced over to make sure that she was not badly hurt.

Matthew's celebratory calls turned to screams as the most enormous grizzly bear, stomped towards him with outstretched paws.

Bowyer Bear towered over Matthew. He chased Matthew around the lake before catching him and tossing the unfortunate boy into the ice-cold waters of the lake. The bear then proceeded to dunk Matthew in and out of the water as though he was a digestive biscuit in a cup of tea.

'Lemme go!' yelled a hoarse Matthew, with his arms and legs kicking wildly.

Bowyer Bear nodded, and with a deep growl picked up the soggy boy, rotated him several times around his head as if he were a rag-doll, and threw the unruly lad into the next cavern and out of sight.

'We'd better go and see what's happened to Matthew' said Delia, with a worried look on her pointed face.

Willow agreed and led the way, however, Matthew was not to be found in the next cavern.

'Oh' said Chiko, with his head cocked to one side, 'I think Bowyer Bear was a little bit too enthusiastic.'

Delia nodded. 'It's time to go back.'

They reappeared in the living room where Matthew was still asleep on the couch.

'I'll wake him up!' hissed Delia. 'Bowyer Bear must have really frightened him.'

'Absolutely marvellous' whistled Chiko. 'A bad, evil boy, kicking our Mischa like that.'

Delia jumped onto Matthew and with her paw, patted his face until he started to wake up.

'Wait. Here comes Mrs. Jennings,' barked Mischa, 'Let's go.'

A short time later, Mrs. Jennings waddled over to the rickety fence as fast as her dumpy legs could carry her. She looked very pale.

'Mischa, oh Oi am so ou' a breath. Mischa, Oi don' know wha's happened' puffed Mrs. Jennings. 'Poor little Matthew woke up from his nap on the sofa in such a state. He was ranting on about animals an' snow an' bears. Oi don't know what's come over him. And then, tha' nice Mrs. Bethel, from down the road came to the door collecting fer the' homeless with her luvely husky dog, an' Matthew went into hysterics when he saw it! He pointed at poor Willow saying tha' she was a freaky monster dog, with her two funny coloured eyes! Why Oi was so embarrassed, an' Mrs. Bethel wa' very upset. Willow growled at Matthew an' wanted to bite him. Then tha' boy started wavin' his arms around and he says this house is haunted!' Mrs. Jennings stopped to mop her brow. 'And then he ran past Mrs. Bethel an' her dog, to the station to catch the next train home without even collecting his bag from the spare room! Oh he ha' giv'n me such a turn. He seemed quite delirious. He refused a cup of tea an' a slice of cake and says he's never coming back. He was rantin' and ravin' 'bout you, a bird an' a cat, an that nice husky dog down the road, takin' him to a cave full o' faeries, and a big bear over seven foot high, tha' threw him into a cold lake wit' rainbow fish in it. "Well Oi never" Oi says to me sister Jemimah, when Oi phoned to say wha' had happened, "Oi'm so sorry, but Oi haven't got a clue wha' Matthew's on about. Don't know why he wanted to travel home all on his own after such a shor' space o' time. Oi just let him have a nap on the couch an' the next thin' he's acting like he's possessed!"'

Mrs. Jennings took a pink hankie to her forehead for another wipe, then bent down and gave Mischa a pat on the head and Delia's ears a stroke. 'Don't know why Oi'd be talkin' to you an' tellin' you all my problems when yo' can't understand wha' Oi'm sayin'.'

'But we can, we can!' whistled Chiko, bouncing up and down excitedly on the fence.

'Wha' a lovely song tha' little robin is singin'!'

'Song?!' muttered Chiko, disgustedly. He frowned and scratched his beak on the fence, left right.

Mrs. Jennings shook her head and placed her hands on her large hips. 'Me sister Jemimah says tha' Matthew rang her and said he never ever wants to come to this 'ouse again.'

'Hooray' cheered Delia.

'No more Matthew Orrible!' added Mischa.

'Finally, we can now have some peace' Chiko chortled. 'Who would have thought that a nice nap could get rid of our visitor.'

Chapter 5: Playing Games.

'Mmmm, Saturday. It's such a bright and breezy day, just the sort of day to get into some mischief' grinned Mischa, as she basked on the immaculate, peppermint green lawn watching her Human-Being pet with amusement. She stretched out her legs, rolled onto her back and wriggled contentedly in the warm, dry grass.

Mrs. Jennings, however, was in a bad mood. A very, bad mood. She had spent most of the morning putting out wet washing and bringing in dry washing, washing up, drying up, ironing, cleaning the kitchen and having to pick up Mischa's toys which littered the house and the garden.

By midday she was fed up. Really fed up. And was not amused by Mischa's doing little or nothing every single day.

'You're getting so lazy. Oi wouldn't be at all surprised if yer legs dropped off from lack of use' she grunted at the sheltie.

'Huh' snorted Mischa.

A stifled laugh came from behind the washing line.

'An' as for you, Delia' continued Mrs. Jennings, grumpily, not even bothering to look up at the cat, 'yer spend so much time washing yerself, keeping yer fur shiny and spotless, Oi'm sure you could make yerself invisible.'

She picked up the pink washing basket and stumped back into the kitchen to put the kettle on.

Delia opened her mouth and shut it again in surprise.

'Wazza matter?' chirped Chiko. 'Cat got your tongue?!'

Chiko looped the loop and laughed at the two girls. 'Tee he he, Mrs Jennings has got it in for the two of you today! One very lazy dog, versus the invisible cat. What a good match that would make.'

'Shut up, Chiko, or you might just find yourself turning into a very long, juicy earthworm! Or just imagine, a poor little bird with vertigo! Now that's something worth thinking about!' Delia stalked off down the garden.

Mischa giggled and rolled around, 'Delia's very catty this morning!'

She spotted a white, straggly, mangy looking cat, scouring the outskirts of the pond searching for a fresh goldfish for lunch.

Mischa put her long nose in the air and sniffed extremely loudly.

'Chiko, can you whiff a funny smell? A stinky, dingy, ditch-water smell? Oh no! It's not an unpleasant aroma. It's Tizzy, the stinky, smelly, alley cat!'

Tizzy looked up and stretched, lazily. She slowly swaggered over to Mischa, with her balding, white tail bent to one side.

'Well, Tizzy, you certainly do give meaning to the phrase "look at what the cat brought in!" I don't know why Mrs. Jennings finds you so appealing!'

Tizzy fluttered her long eyelashes and managed to wink and twinkle her eyes at the same time.

'It's because I'm so cute and loveable. Human-Being pets just have to give me lots of food, because they think Ms. Amelia is a mean, horrid, Human-Being pet. She never feeds me the food that I want. All I get is disgusting chunks in a tin that's only fit for mutts like you. Ms. Amelia is wicked, and shortly she'll pay dearly.'

'What?!' exclaimed Mischa, unable to believe her ears. 'Ms. Amelia is the kindest Human-Bean pet in Midsomer-Atte-Stoke, apart from Mrs. Jennings of course.'

Tizzy laughed, and strutted up and down with her tail in the air. 'You dogs are so stupid, you can't even see past your long dribbling noses.

Mrs. Jennings opened the back door and trotted out with half a sandwich. 'Tizzy, Tizzy my pet, how are yer? Oi saw yer from the kitchen window and thought yer might like some of me sardine sandwich.'

Tizzy meowed pitifully and then, as if on cue, purred and walked in and out of Mrs. Jennings' dumpy legs, with her scrawny white tail erect, like a submarine's periscope.

'Sounds like a bleedin' motor boat' scoffed Mischa. 'She's so full of herself. What that cat needs is a good kick up the rump! How dare she make herself at home in my garden.' She stuck her snout in the air in disgust.

'Mischa, don't growl at Tizzy. Aah now. Look how 'ungry the poor kitty is' said Mrs. Jennings, stroking Tizzy's flea ridden coat.

'Oh cut the cat-pooh, Tizzy' grunted Mischa. 'Go and wash yourself you smelly cat.'

'Mischa!' exclaimed Mrs. Jennings, sternly. 'Don't be so stroppy. An' stop tha' snarling.'

'Got to go, fat-face' screeched Tizzy.

'Bite my tail!' retorted Mischa rudely.

'I will get under your fur later, my little dog. P.S. tell Mrs. Jennings that I would prefer freshly baked salmon for my tea. Those sardines were so tasteless.'

Mischa growled and snapped as Tizzy leaped onto Mr. Barrowclough's fence and out of sight.

'I could have had that sandwich. Stinky, smelly alley cat' raged Mischa.

Jumping up and banging her front paws on Mr. Barrowclough's fence, she barked, menacingly, 'Don't enter my garden again!'

'Mischa, Oi won't tolerate tha' bad behaviour. If yer not a good girl, Oi won't bake banana cake fer you!' grunted Mrs. Jennings, as she marched back to the kitchen.

'That cat never looks clean. It always looks and smells as though it's rolled in something disgusting!'

'How right you are!' said Delia, creeping out from under the conifer.

'Have you been there all this time?' asked Mischa, with her head cocked to one side, inquisitively.

'Lady business' replied Delia coyly.

'What! In my garden. Purlease!'

'Oh come on! Let's go down to the Tamarix and see what adventure the magic shrub has in store for us today.'

The three friends sat under the Tamarix. Delia took a small reed pipe out from behind her ear and played an eerie tune.

Chiko looked gob smacked. 'I didn't know you could play music.'

'Ah.' Delia purred. 'There's a lot of things you don't know about me.'

'Can you make yourself invisible? Really invisible so that you can get up to mischief and do lots of funny stuff and have all kinds of horrendously weird things happen?' said Mischa, waving her paws around.

Delia stretched. 'I can do anything with my magic. Anything at all.' She played another line of the strange tune. Chiko whistled along with her playing.

The slow air went on for another few minutes.

Chiko gave a loud yawn and put his head under his wing.

Mischa could not help but yawn, also. 'That tune is making me sleepy.' She closed one eye, and then the other, whilst Delia continued playing the reed pipe.

The dreamlike music continued and Mischa smiled in her sleep.

Suddenly, they were woken up to extremely loud roaring.

'What's happening?' said Mischa, totally startled by the commotion.

'Ah ha!' Delia rubbed her paws together with glee. 'This is a Premiership football stadium.' Chiko and Mischa looked at her with blank faces.

'Premiership football! Football! Come on you two! Surely you can remember that game where Human-Being pets run around like lunatics kicking a round, bouncy thing called a ball?'

Mischa slowly nodded her head. 'I've often seen Bruno the Boxer doing something similar with his Human-Bean pet.'

'Being, Mischa. They are not vegetable seeds' huffed Delia.

The three friends watched the two teams of men running up and down the grass pitch. The huge stadium was filled to capacity with equally mad fans. On the left side banners, hats and scarves waved frantically in the air by fans wearing the blue jerseys of Weatherton United. To the right, there was a mass of red scarves, hats and flags, together with the red jerseys of Riverpool Athletic fans.

The noise was terrific, with both sets of fans singing, chanting, blowing trumpets, banging drums, geeing on their players and generally making such a loud din that Mischa joined in with long high pitched howling.

'Come down here and stand on the sideline' said Delia. 'Don't worry. Nobody can see us. We are now invisible.'

'No way!' barked Mischa, excitedly jumping up and down on the sideline.

'Yes, we truly are' said Chiko, nipping the linesman on his ear and watching him flap his arms in the air.

They watched the match for a while. Players raced up and down the pitch. They dribbled, passed the ball between themselves, and very occasionally, took a shot, which was often not even near the goalposts. In fact, it was a very boring match, and the fans were becoming restless.

Mischa ran up and down the sideline, watching eagerly.

'Over here. Quickly. Pass the ball! Get out of my way, Andrews' screamed a Riverpool player, his eyes blazing with anger.

'Ouch! You'll be sorry you kicked me in the leg, Brady.' Andrews retorted.

'No I won't. Now give me the ball, it's my throw in' yelled Smith. He grabbed the ball off of Butch Brady.

'You wait. Ger outa me way or I'll knock all yer teeth out.' Butch Brady's eyes held Smith in a stare. He then picked him up, and threw him onto the ground as though he weighed as much as a bag of rice.

Next followed a free-for-all punch-up between two Riverpool and two Weatherton players. As they fought, their arms and legs flew in all directions like a giant sized windmill. Meanwhile some team-mates ran over to the scuffle and tried to pull the four fighters apart.

The linesman, who stood in the wrong place at the wrong time, managed to receive a punch on the nose.

Mischa watched the match with amazement, barking and jumping up and down on the sideline. 'Let's join in! Let's create our own melee!'

'It's like a big, big battle' twittered Chiko, shaking his head from side to side. 'We birds never conduct ourselves with such downright disgraceful behaviour.' And with that final comment, he flew on to the pitch and landed on Jack Andrew's head, and pulled the player's hair with his beak.

'This is fun!' Mischa ran onto the pitch and circled the referee. 'Over here, over here, throw me the ball, Human-Bean!' Mischa bounced up and down, trying to dislodge the ball from the referee's hand, whilst he continued to blow his whistle and wave a red card over his head like a possessed man.

Mr. Duffie couldn't believe his eyes. He had never had to referee a match with so many defiant players. He blew his whistle, peep-peeping for all he was worth, and waving the red card with the intention of sending off two players; but to no avail. Nobody paid him any attention. Nobody listened to his whistle or had any intention of walking off the pitch.

Suddenly the ball was snatched from out of his hand. Mr. Duffie was furious.

'How dare you' he screamed at the players. But then he saw that the ball was making its way up the field. On its own! The only player left on that side of the pitch was the Riverpool Athletic goalkeeper, who was also scratching his head and watching the football, bounce and dribble along the grass by itself.

Weatherton United fans roared with delight, and waved on the football, which was rolling along the grass, unaided.

Mischa was delighted, too. She dribbled the football with her nose, bounced it with her front paws and made her way up to the Riverpool goal.

Parkie, the Riverpool Athletic goalkeeper, came out of the goalmouth and tried to kick the ball back up the pitch. But Mischa was not going to have that! She made the ball circle Parkie, several times. Faster and faster, he turned around in circles, watching the ball. Parkie became dizzy, and staggered around in a daze. He looked like a giant octopus, with arms waving in all directions. The Weatherton United fans could only laugh at him, hysterically.

'Ha ha! Look at Parkie! He's running around in circles. That ball is gonna go into the net! That's a magic ball and we're gonna a score a goal! GOAL!'

The Weatherton Athletic fans roared with delight. They waved their flags and banners and sang until their throats were raw.

Mischa jumped up and down, then ran back down the pitch and nosed the

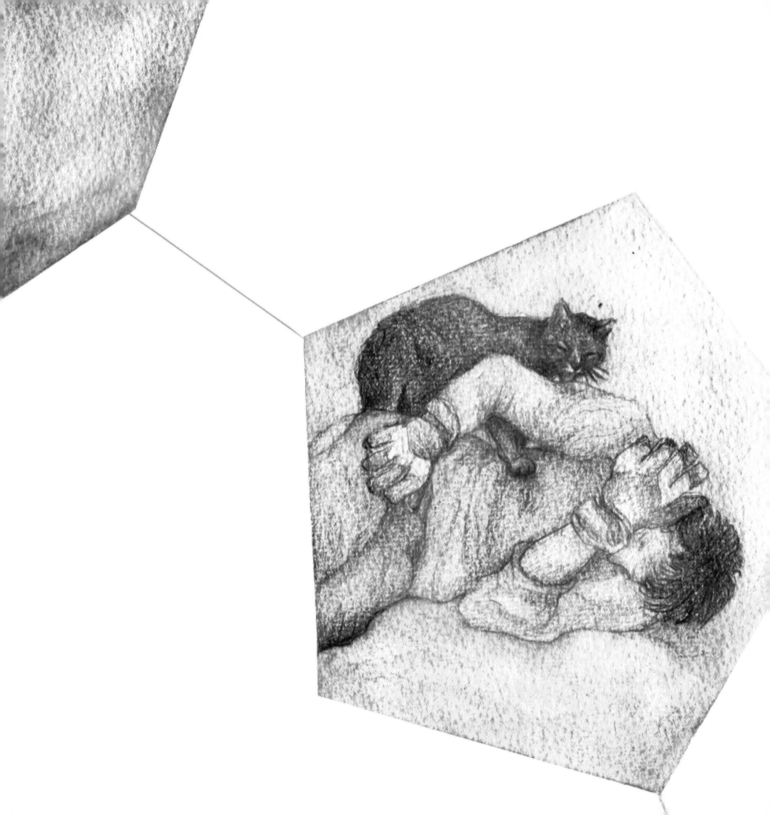

ball into the Weatherton United goal, this time making the Riverpool fans roar with delight.

The referee and players stopped fighting and looked around. The ball clearly had a mind of its own.

There was peck on Brady's ear and he roared angrily, waving his arms wildly about his head.

Delia jumped on to the Weatherton goalkeeper, and whilst pinning him down with her front paws, licked his face with her rough pink tongue.

'Ah! There's a ghost, there's a ghost! Get it off me!' screamed Freddy Grant, the goalkeeper.

Both groups of fans could not believe their eyes. The referee, both sets of players and the linesmen were behaving very strangely, indeed. The ball was doing its own thing, players were running around waving their arms in the air, Freddy Grant, the Weatherton United goalkeeper was pinned to the ground with his legs kicking wildly.

'Peep, peep.' Mr. Duffie blew his whistle again and again. And for his efforts, Chiko rewarded him with a peck on the nose.

'Ow ow ow' shouted the referee. 'Abandon the match! Abandon the match!'

The crowd chanted a chorus of boos. 'This is the first decent match we've seen all season!' they screamed in unison.

Delia walked back down to the sideline. 'Mischa, Chiko. Something is not quite right with these Human-Beings. I'd better consult with C.A.T. Come on, I think we've had enough fun for one day.'

'Oh no, Delia' wailed the sheltie. 'I like this game! It's so much more fun than playing "where's the bone?" with itchy Mac.'

'Mischa! Chiko! Now!' screeched Delia.

'Ok' said Chiko, giving two final playful nips to Andrews.

Mischa dribbled the ball over to a linesman and with a push from her front paws, made him topple over like a clown.

'So much fun and so little time to play' moaned Mischa.

'I remember when Mrs. Jennings took Marnie-Rae and I to the seaside in her rusty, red machine on wheels. We walked on the beach and had ice cream and then saw a funny show just like that match.'

'A funny show?' enquired Delia, who knew everything yet did not have a clue what Mischa was talking about.

'Yes, yes. A show. With a big red box covered with a big stripy curtain around it, with puppets hitting each other with pretend sausages.'

'Ah' said Delia, nodding her head, finally understanding. 'You mean, the players in this match reminded you of a Punch and Judy show.'

'Yes, yes!' barked Mischa. 'This was an extra funny version of a Punch and Judy show; we were the stars! I bet Mrs. Jennings would've loved to see me dribble that ball up the field and score two goals. Oh I'm so very clever.'

'Humph' said Chiko. 'Self-praise is no praise. Besides, I got to have lots more fun by pulling hair and nipping so many noses.'

'Now now, children. No more squabbling. It's time for Mischa to go back home and help Mrs. Jennings around the garden.' Delia lifted her paw and itched her face, thoughtfully. 'There's definitely something strange happening in Human-Being land. I'll have to discuss this with C.A.T.'

'Nah! They're normal' chirped Chiko, cheerfully. 'Those Human-Being pets always act as though they're stupid!' He tucked one of his ruffled feathers back into place. 'That's just their nature.'

'Mischa' called Mrs. Jennings. 'Mischa! Where are yer?'

'Couldn't possibly move a muscle. Much too tired. Must sleep' murmured Mischa.

'Mischa! Mischa, get up yer lazy dog. Pick up yer toys and bring them back into the kitchen. Now!' barked an impatient Mrs. Jennings.

Mischa opened one eye and peered wearily around. That was such an excellent dream, but with such a rude awakening. She stretched lazily and raised herself up from under the Tamarix.

Chiko and Delia were sitting on the rickety fence, admiring how loudly such a small dog could snore.

'Did you enjoy your afternoon, Mischa?' enquired Delia.

'I thought I was dreaming' said the sheltie.

'I have a present for you' purred Delia, delightedly.

'What's that?'

A shrill peep peep,from a whistle nearly bowled Mischa over with fright.

Chiko fell off the fence in hoots of laughter.

'Mischa! Mischa!' Peep peep blew Mrs. Jennings on the whistle.

'No rest for the good puppy' muttered Mischa as she rounded up her toys, bounded and for the kitchen door. After dumping them in the kitchen, she spotted something bright in the garden, near the climbing honeysuckle. She headed back out and picked up the bright pink and white flag, just like the ones they were waving in the stands of the football match.

Mischa seized the giant flag and ran around the garden with her pink and white banner, flying it in the air like a giant sized kite. She pretended she had just scored a goal.

'Whoo-hoo, look at me! Goal!' she cried out delightedly, as she tossed the flag in to the air. 'Goal!'

'I wouldn't do that if I were you' said a sniggering Chiko at the height of his whisper.

'Why ever not' replied Mischa, grumpily. 'You're always trying to spoil my fun. I don't care, this is my flag and I'm going to score another goal!'

'Mischa! Mischa!' Peep peep peep bellowed Mrs. Jennings, as loudly as a giant, disco speaker.

Mischa stopped dead in her tracks and looked up at Mrs. Jennings with the pink and white flag in her mouth.

Mrs. Jennings stood in front of Mischa, crossly with her hands on her hips.

'Mischa! Just what do yer think yer doing with me knickers?!'

Chapter 6: More Banana Cake

Mischa cleared her throat and began warming up her voice with an arpeggio. 'Ahem ahem. Bow wow wow wow, bow wow wow wow' She shook her head from side to side. She started on her scales. 'Do re mi fa so la ti do. Do re mi fa so la ti dooooooooo.'

'Give it a rest, Mischa' whistled Chiko. 'You're giving me an earache!'

Mischa scowled at him and cleared her throat again. 'Mrs. Jennings is going to enter me into "The Perfect Pooch" competition, and I'm going to sing a brand new song that I composed myself.' She nodded to confirm that it was an original piece.

Chiko sat on a swaying rowan branch and prepared himself for a headache, and a laugh.

'Oh I am such a lovely girl, I really don't know why.
Oh I am such a lovely girl...'

Chiko interrupted with 'Your singing makes me want to die!' Mischa glared at him and continued singing.

'I can sing my A, B, Cs.'

'And then I'll watch you scratch your fleas!' finished Chiko, roaring with laughter.

'Mischa, Mischa' wailed Mrs. Jennings, racing from the back door as fast as her chubby legs could carry her. 'Oi heard you howlin' an' thought yer had a pain in yer belly, or somethin' worse. Are yer all right my love?' She patted Mischa's head.

Mischa looked at her in disgust. 'I was singing my latest song' she barked, stamping her foot in anger. She lifted her long snout into the air and began the song, again.

Chiko danced from leg to leg on the swaying branch. Mrs. Jennings looked at Mischa and then at Chiko with a frown on her round face.

After two verses of her latest song, Mischa took a bow.

'Ah' said Mrs. Jennings. 'You're singing.'

'And so the penny's dropped' muttered Mischa, caustically.

Chiko whistled a little ditty himself.

'A duet' cried Mrs. Jennings, clasping her hands in delight.

'No, no, no' barked Mischa, stamping her foot over and over again. 'I want to sing alone. And since when is Chiko a pooch, anyway?'

Chiko nearly fell off the branch with laughter.

'Ah Chiko, my pet. Oi can't enter you as duet with Mischa, cos yer not a little dog.'

Mischa shook her head from side to side. 'So big, and yet so slow.'

'Although,' continued Mrs. Jennings, 'Oi could fabricate a little something to disguise you as a little dog.'

Mischa had visions of Chiko running around in a furry suit wagging a made up tail. 'Well, Chiko, you could look like a mini poodle with a pretty red bow in your hair.'

'Oh shut up you silly dog. Who's going to want to listen to you howling like a banshee in any case.'

'I do,' smiled Delia, creeping out from under the rose bush.

'Delia, my lovely kitty. What a shiny coat yer've got. Oi bet yer can sing beautifully, too' said Mrs. Jennings, bending down to stroke a perfect no-hair-out-of-place groomed cat.

'Mischa, sing your song again so that we can all enjoy your voice' purred Delia.

Mischa cleared her throat again. 'Ahem.

Oh I am such a lovely girl, I really don't know why.
Oh I am such a lovely girl, I'm going to make you sigh.
With my beautiful voice, you haven't got much choice,
But to listen and sing-along too.
Oh I am such a lovely girl I really don't know why,
Oh I am such a lovely girl, my singing will make you cry,
With happiness, and laughter,
You can join in, do,
I can sing you pretty lullabies,
And dance the Fandango, too.'

Mrs. Jennings jumped up and down with delight. 'Mischa, tha' t'was truly wonderful. Yer must enter "The Perfect Pooch" competition. Wasn't she wonderful? Isn't she the most perfect dog on this planet?' Mrs. Jennings applauded her pet loudly.

Chiko muffled a giggle while Delia beamed widely.

Tizzy jumped over the fence. 'Did I hear someone crying with pain? Mischa, are you not feeling well? Was that *you*, screeching and howling?' Tizzy scoffed loudly and put her paw down her throat, pretended to be sick.

Mischa raced over to Tizzy and growled at her nose to nose, baring her teeth, menacingly. 'We all know you're a stinky troublemaker.'

Tizzy's eyes glowered purple for a split second before changing back to green. Mischa, not knowing what she saw, passed this off as feeling faint from over-singing!

'Go away! Go away!' barked Mischa.

'Smell you later. Mutt.' and with that, Tizzy strutted off.

'Mischa. Stop barking at tha' poor little cat. Now. Oi must go back in and get ready for shopping. Don't be long, it's going to rain.'

The sky quickly became overcast. A huge broody, bruised, black coloured cloud loomed overhead. Mischa ran back inside the house and found Mrs. Jennings putting on her green macintosh and yellow scarf. She placed the extra large umbrella at the front door.

'Come in to ta' kitchen my darling, I've made you a nice bowl of warm tea and I've just baked your favourite banana cake. And here' she reached up and cut a large slice of cake and put it in Mischa's dish, 'is an extra large slice fer you.'

She picked up her glasses from the kitchen counter and popped them into her handbag 'Oi won't be long. Oi'm just going down to the shop and Oi'll be straight back to see yer. Oi'm sorry to leave you alone in the house when there might be a storm. Oi know that you don't like thunder.' She bent down, patted her little dog on the head, grabbed her umbrella and headed out of the door.

Mischa wagged her tail and licked her lips. The scent of freshly baked banana cake wafted to the sheltie's snout. 'Mmmm. Delicious.'

Mischa drank some tea and was just about to take a large chunk out of her mouth-watering banana cake, when she heard two loud bumps.

'That's not thunder' she thought. She ran to the front door in case it were a burglar and barked sharply, but there was nobody there.

Mischa then ran to the French windows at the back of the house and barked again. But she still could not see anyone. She gave a sigh and thought she had been hearing things. She walked back to the kitchen and had another slurp of warm tea.

Suddenly, there was a tap on her shoulder. Mischa got such a fright that she lifted the bowl up with her snout and spilt tea over the floor.

Mischa turned around sharply and found Chiko and Delia laughing.

'What did you do that for? It's rude and bold to give me a fright' she snapped, angrily. 'And Mrs. J. will be furious when she sees this mess.'

'Oh don't worry about such trivial manners, my dear dog' purred Delia, carefully washing soot off her paws.

'Pooh' said Mischa, frowning crossly. 'Mrs. Jennings will not be pleased. What happened to the two of you? You're dirty!'

'We came down the chimney,' said Chiko, scratching his beak on a dining room chair, 'Mrs. J. forgot to leave the window open.'

Just then, a bright flash of lightning lit up the room, followed by an almighty crash of thunder.

'Ooh,' cried Mischa, her whole body quaking, 'I must hide in my bed.'

'What for?' said Chiko. 'It's only thunder and lightning, not an army waiting to gun you down. There's absolutely nothing to worry about.'

'Of course there's nothing to worry about, Mischa. Come with us on a magic game, and you can escape this weather' meowed Delia.

'But it's only ten o'clock in the morning' replied the sheltie. 'All the same, I think I'd rather be out on an adventure than sitting here on my own listening to this awful thunder.'

'Good' said Delia, picking up a piece of Tamarix branch, adorned with lovely pink flowers. 'Let us begin.'

They sat down in the middle of the living room, and crossed their legs in the semi-lotus position. Another flash of lightning and an even louder rumble of thunder rang out across the picturesque village. Delia grasped Mischa's paw tightly, and with the other paw, held the pink Tamarix branch on which Chiko was perched, over their heads, sprinkling them with herbal dust. Delia commenced the magic spell.

'Magic far as the eye can see,
Take us back in history,
To a land where man has never been,
Where life is slow and in between.'

Just then, an ear-splitting crash of thunder roared out as though it was a shot fired from a missile launcher. The three friends vanished.

When they reappeared, they found themselves in a vast swamp. Tree roots, mud, vegetation and muck as far as the eye could see.

'Where are we?' shuddered Mischa, as her paws sank into the thick, sticky mud. 'I don't think I like it here.'

'Don't be such a coward, we've only just arrived,' said Delia with a sigh. 'Look. My paws are also muddy, and I spend far more time than you washing and cleaning my fur.'

Chiko decided it was safer to fly than to cling onto Mischa's back, which was wobbling from side to side in the stodgy mud and very much in danger of capsizing completely. He flew ahead and waited on a gnarled, bare tree for the other two slowpokes to catch up.

Just then, an enormous bird, with at least a thirty-foot wingspan, screeched madly and flew out of the sky. It screamed at Chiko and flew directly at the poor robin, who could only gulp in disbelief as he watched the wide gaping beak aiming for him.

Chiko almost died of fright. He managed to save himself by darting into a hole in the tree trunk, as the monstrous bird crashed into the tree and bent its beak. As it stood at the base of the tree, it continued to scream viciously at Chiko.

Delia rushed over to the bird, waving her paws and uttering magic spells.

To Chiko's relief, the bird quit taunting him and flew off.

'Gosh. That was close. That bird nearly had me for dinner' said the robin, mopping his brow with a blue and white spotted handkerchief.

'That was a Terrorsaurus' preached Delia, 'and believe me, that you, a mere robin, would not even have filled his big toe!'

'Delia! Don't be catty! Poor Chiko had a terrible fright' said Mischa, licking Chiko on his beak.

'Ugh' muttered Chiko, wiping his beak with his well-worn hanky.

'Okay, we must stick together and be very, very careful. This is The Valley of the Dinosaurs.'

'Dinosaurs?' stuttered Mischa. 'Delia, haven't you got any sense bringing us here. This place is dangerous and, er, shouldn't dinosaurs be extinct. Why have you brought us here? Oh no we're doomed to die. We're doomed to be eaten alive.' She raised her snout in the air, and howled loudly and pitifully.

'Do be quiet, Mischa' said Chiko. 'It isn't that bad. We've just gone back in time, just for a little while.'

'You see, Mischa, I must find my magic cloak. I left in it a cave near here, many, many years ago. The time has come for me to wear this cloak, for C.A.T. is expecting me to assist him in a dangerous project' purred Delia, regally. 'Just follow me and do as I say, and, if we do come across any dinosaurs, you can be sure that my magic powers will take control of the situation.' She nodded with authority. 'Ah, there goes a stegosaurus. It's such a cumbersome creature, mind you, I'm glad we are not going to get a lift on his back; just look at the size of those plates!'

Mischa and Delia squished through the greeny-brown gunk, with Chiko clinging onto Mischa's back for dear life. Progress was very slow and tedious. After struggling through the swamp for another while, they came within sight of a dense forest. It was thick with grotesquely contorted trees, gnarled into unusual shapes. The forest loomed, menacingly, with lightning piercing the sky.

'Somehow I think I would have been far safer staying at home, eating my slice of banana cake' thought Mischa, aloud.

'Don't be silly, this is fun' chuckled Delia, shaking a lump of mud off her tail. 'Good. Here we are.'

'What do you mean?' asked Mischa. 'I can't see anything. There's nothing here except that big ugly forest and this mass of pongy water between it and us. And look at that mega poopy log floating on it! Trust you to get us lost.'

'My dear dog, we are not lost. And that is not a log. It's Tiny. Tiny the diplodocus' smirked Delia.

'Tiny? Are you demented, Delia? That thing is huge. He must be at least ninety feet long' wailed Mischa, shuddering with fear as the log raised itself slowly out of the water and drew himself out to his full length.

'Don't worry. My magic will take care that Tiny will ferry us safely across the lake. And don't forget, he doesn't eat meat, so you don't have to worry about his belly being hungry.'

Chiko covered his eyes with his wings and anchored his feet to Mischa's collar.

'What have I left myself in for' whined the sheltie.

'Diplodocus, diplodocus, rise out of the lake,
Ferry us safely and try not to make,
Any loud sounds that might awaken the snake,
This I ask of you, Tiny, The Great.'

Tiny gently lifted his head out of the water and smiled at Delia. His long, long neck extended for several yards followed by his gigantic body, which looked far too big and too long for his little minuscule head. Next appeared his tail, which was tremendously long, and covered in slimy leaves. The dinosaur waded easily through the watery mud and bowed to Delia.

'Gosh. He's really, really big' uttered Mischa.

'Yes' whispered Chiko, with his wings still covering his face.

Tiny lowered his enormous tail to where the three friends were waiting, like a huge drawbridge.

'Come along' sang Delia, as she marched up the long tail and onto Tiny's back. 'What are you waiting for?'

Chiko groaned loudly as Mischa started the long walk up Tiny's tail. She slid a couple of times and nearly fell off.

'Mischa! Get a grip' shouted Chiko.

'Oops. Sorry' said Mischa as she clambered up beside Delia.

'Now, hold on tightly. We don't want anyone falling off!' commanded Delia.

They held on as tightly as they could as Tiny waded through the murky waters. The journey across to the forest was slow and bumpy. Chiko peered out through his wings and saw the size of the huge fish swimming along side with their teeth baring ominously, hoping for one of the passengers to fall into the swamp. 'Help me! Daisy! Oh where are you Daisy when I need you?' he cried.

Delia laughed. 'Chiko, you're such a girl!'

When they eventually arrived at the other side of the swampy lake, Tiny gently lowered his neck onto the land, and the three friends edged their way down his neck, and his head, and over his nose.

Mischa ran off as fast as she could with Chiko still attached to her fur. Delia bowed to Tiny and thanked him most sincerely. Tiny bowed back, graciously, and bellowed loudly.

The grass, near the thick forest, was a luscious shade of green. Mischa skipped and jumped happily. She then rolled over and over in the grass, ridding herself off the slimy mud. 'I bet there aren't any dinosaurs here' she sang, happily.

'Yes, you are correct' replied Delia. 'Follow me to the cave. That's where we will find the magic cloak.'

After another long walk through the gloomy forest, where it felt as though hundreds of probing eyes were watching their every move, they reached a small black cave.

Mischa peeped in. 'It's very dark. I don't like the dark.' She followed Delia, cautiously.

As they entered the cave, the darkness was transformed into a glittering spectacle. Thousands upon thousands of tiny lights flickered around the cave, making it warm and friendly. Each light winked and sparkled, as if by magic.

'Wow' said Mischa. 'There must be millions of faeries in here.'

'Those little faeries are, in fact, glowworms' said Delia.

'Wow' Mischa repeated, gazing around the cave and walking round and round in circles, with her mouth wide open.

Delia walked to the back of the cave, and with great difficulty, moved a large grey boulder. There she uncovered a very old wooden chest, embedded in the wall. She pulled out the chest and slowly opened the dusty lid, removing several pieces of gold and silver, ranging from candleholders to coins, to large ornate cups. Underneath the witch's hat, and the willow wand, she reached down and pulled out the ancient cloak.

'Ah! I haven't seen this for forty thousand years' purred Delia, delightedly pulling out the cloak and brushing it against her face.

'Forty thousand years' exclaimed Mischa and Chiko in unison.

'Cats don't live that long.'

'But magic cats do' smiled Delia, seemingly clutching air. In reality, her paws were delicately stroking a material, so finely woven, that only appeared to be a cape when examined closely.

'Humph' said Chiko. 'You're so vain. And old!'

Delia closed the chest and replaced the boulder. The three friends left the cave armed with the cloak. The glowworms blinked out one by one, leaving the cave in darkness, once again.

It had been raining steadily since the three friends had entered the cave. The sky had darkened and echoes of distant rumbling thunder could be heard. They walked to a muddy clearing in the forest. Mischa looked around the surrounding forest, scrutinising the area. She still felt as though eyes were watching and waiting. Her fur stood on end.

A giant snake, whose body was thicker than any tree trunk, slid out slyly from behind the trees, taking Delia, Chiko and Mischa completely by surprise. The Takoda quivered nervously.

Its purple and green diamond emblazoned body slid along the forest floor and its head swooped swiftly at Delia through the torrential rain, baring its fangs and lunging its silver forked tongue, angrily.

Delia gracefully evaded the attack. 'This is Sneerahraje, King of all Squamata and Dark Magician of this forest.'

'What does he want?' whimpered Mischa, wishing she could just close her eyes and reappear back under the Tamarix, or better still, in her bed with that enormous slice of banana cake along side.

'Sneerahraje wants my magic cloak. But he is not going to have it. This is my cloak. It belongs to me, Delia, great Magician of Maybola.'

'Delia, is your magic stronger than the snake's?' asked Chiko, frightened of the consequences.

'We'll have to wait and see' she replied. 'This is a deadly snake who has killed many great Takoda in the past. Hide under that small bush over there, and under no circumstances are you to come out until I say so.'

Mischa and Chiko took cover and watched the encounter from under a shrub.

Delia wrapped the cloak around her shoulders and became invisible. She reappeared to the right of the snake, dressed in gold plated armour and carrying a large golden sword with a pulsing red stone in the hilt. Delia lifted the sword, swung it, and severed the snake in two.

The giant snaked hissed and screamed.

She was just about to strike again when Sneerahraje slithered out in two directions, becoming separate snakes, each as deadly as the original. Their heads, contorted and twisted with hostility, turned from side to side, watching the cat with hatred dripping from each deadly eye.

In a flash, the two Sneerahrajes breathed fire at Delia, and lucky for her, the armour reflected the heat and scorched both snakes making them scream in pain.

Delia retreated several paces, giving herself room to think.

The two snakes then turned into one giant bat, which flew at Delia, viciously trying to bite through her armour.

Delia spread herself on the floor of the forest, and remained perfectly still.

Just as the giant bat swooped down for the kill, Delia turned herself into a bottomless hole. The bat fell in and the devious cat covered the hole with a huge black boulder. The bat screeched and roared, trying to tear aside the mighty stone, but without success.

Delia was relieved, but just when she thought the whole episode was over,

Sneerahraje turned itself into an almighty jet of water, which lifted up the boulder high into the sky, and threw it aside as though it were a pebble.

The magic water then transformed into a giant, three-horned gorilla with lizards feet. Bounding ferociously towards the cat, the giant gorilla squashed plants, bugs and bushes, in its path.

Delia, who dug deep inside for extra energy, turned herself into a giant scorpion with an extra long tail that was razor sharp. She was huge.

As the three-horned gorilla rushed towards Delia, she threw herself at its neck, stinging and stunning the creature, such that when it crashed to the ground, it was instantly slain and disappeared.

The silence in the Dark Forest was deafening.

The scorpion looked around carefully, making sure that Sneerahraje was gone.

Delia transformed herself back into a cat and folded the magic cloak, carefully. She called to Mischa and Chiko, and encouraged them to come out from their hiding place.

'Is it over?' whispered Chiko, still shaking with fright.

'Yes. That monster is gone, at least for now. Sneerahraje is temporarily trounced, but he will be back for this cape' Delia said, leading them back into the clearing.

'Hooray for Delia' cheered Chiko and Mischa. 'Thank the great C.A.T. it's all over!' They were very relieved.

The storm moved away and the rain stopped. In its place, the sun beamed and shone. A large rainbow arched over the forest. The luscious green vegetation smelled sweet and inviting in the warm sunshine. Mischa looked up and saw bananas hanging from a nearby tree and sniffed the air contently.

The sheltie woke up to find herself inside her living room. She raced over to the French windows and peered out, making sure that there were no dinosaurs lurking in the garden, and then turned abruptly as she remembered her banana cake in the kitchen.

Just then, Mrs. Jennings opened the front door.

'Mischa! Mischa! Oi'm home. Were you frightened by the thunder?'

'Of course not' barked Mischao batting her tail up and down, because it was always exciting to welcome home Mrs. Jennings when she returned from the shops.

'Oi've got a surprise for you' she said, patting the little dog's head.

'Yes! Yes!' she barked, delightedly. The sheltie stood on her hind legs and danced for Harriet Jennings.

'Mac has come to visit.'

'Oh no, not again' groaned the sheltie, landing back heavily, on all fours.

The little black Scottish terrier poked his head out from the kitchen

'Mischa, ma wee lassie, ma Winch! It's great to see ye again. I hope yer feelin' better.

The last time I saw ye, ye couldnae eat yer birthday cake, and I suppose ur cannae eat this slice of banana cake either.' He gobbled up the large, moist slice of cake with gusto. He slobbered his tongue over the crumbs remaining on his grey whiskers, and gave her a big wink.

'His Winch! The cheek of him. And he was never meant to eat that piece of banana cake' grumbled Mischa.

Chapter 7: The Magic Skates

Later that evening, when it was almost time for bed, Mrs. Jennings, wearing her favourite pink fluffy dressing gown with matching pink slippers, topped with green bows, gave Mischa a bowl of frothy hot chocolate with two white marshmallows.

'Sweet dreams, Mischa. Oi'll see yer in the morning.'

'Goodnight Mrs. J.' yipped Mischa, finishing off her chocolate, climbing into bed and tucking her paws under her chin.

Mrs. Jennings locked the front door, turned off the downstairs lights and trundled up the stairs, noisily.

Mischa stretched out her paws, and within seconds, fell into a deep sleep.

It was a lovely, relaxing sleep, and she was really enjoying the rest after such a long hectic day.

'Yelp' she cried, suddenly, sitting up abruptly and staring around whilst wildly rubbing her nose.

'Chiko? Chiko! Did you peck my nose?'

Chiko grinned, cheekily, excitedly hopping backwards and forwards.

'What are you doing here?' she whispered. 'Don't you know that Mrs. Jennings is upstairs?'

'I'm not that stupid' chirped the robin.

'But she could come down the stairs at any minute' hissed Mischa.

'No. Mrs. J. is asleep.'

'But why are you here? Is Delia sick?'

'Of course not. How can a magic cat get sick? Delia is here, too. She's in the living room. We're going to play a magic game and thought you might like to come along.'

'What! At this time of night!' said Mischa, horrified at the thought of missing any more sleep. She got up, reluctantly, and followed Chiko into the living room, stretching her back legs as she walked.

'Mischa' drawled Delia, jumping off the sofa and walking over to the fireplace.

'Normally I sleep during the day, so maybe, just this once, I would like to go somewhere in the middle of the night. After all, we often play our magic games by day to accommodate your ridiculous sleeping habits.'

'Ooh' said Mischa. 'Okay, but Mrs. Jennings will go potty when she finds that I am missing. She will think that I've been dognapped.'

'Mrs. Jennings,' smiled Delia, sweetly, 'is fast asleep, and will remain so until eight-thirty tomorrow morning. Besides, my little pooch, who would want to dognap you?'

'Huh' she snorted, 'but how are we going to play if the Tamarix is outside and we're stuck in here?' mumbled Mischa, edging backwards towards her nice, warm, inviting bed.

'No problem, my furry pal, just like the last time, I've brought a tiny branch of the feathery tree into the house. Honestly, Mischa, your excuses are getting lamer and lamer.'

'Sit on the floor next to me, and Delia will cast her magic spell' stated Chiko, to convince her friends.

They sat down together, in the semi-lotus position, with Delia holding the Tamarix branch. She sprinkled orange powder over them and whispered:

'Magic in the dead of night,
Take us far and out of sight,
To a cold, cold place where people go,
To enjoy themselves without any snow.'

The three friends drifted upwards, melting through the ceiling. When they reappeared, they found themselves in a huge, cold stadium.

It was an ice-skating rink, crammed with people chattering noisily.

At one end of the stadium sat several men and women, wearing figure hugging skating costumes in an array of different colours. Some designs were so magnificent and sparkly, that Mischa could not take her eyes off of them, and stared in amazement.

'Ooh' said Mischa. 'Those Human-Bean dresses are so pretty. I really like that orange one with the ruffles and frills and sequins and ribbons, and, what's that?' her mouth started watering. 'Is that the biggest basket of chocolates, sweets, lollypops, fruit and cake that I have ever seen? I do believe it is!' Her eyes nearly popped out with the excitement and greediness. She licked her lips and rubbed her belly, hungrily. 'Mmmm.'

'The winner of this skating competition will win that great big hamper' said Delia, watching Mischa's tongue hang out in a drooling mess.

Chiko fluttered about in amazement. 'Super duper! Delia, are there skates made for dogs and robins?' he enquired, tilting his head to the right and hopping up and down on one foot.

'Of course you can have a go at winning the prize. That's why I've brought you here. In fact, I've already entered the two of you in the singles figure skating competition.'

'What!' exclaimed Chiko. 'But we can't skate and we haven't got fancy costumes.'

'Well, I suppose I shall have to call upon my magic to help you out' purred Delia, stroking her whiskers.

She clicked her claws together and the lights of the stadium were extinguished to yield an eerie darkness. Fortunately, they were relit only moments later, and when they came back on again, Mischa was seen to be adorned with a sparkling silver bow, a matching silver sequin dress with puffed sleeves, and a small pair of white ice skates.

Chiko was dressed in an all-in-one navy blue suit, with gold ribbon around the edges. On his claws, the tiniest pair of black ice skates ever imaginable, glistened.

'Magnificent' exclaimed Chiko.

'Stunning! Thank you, Delia' said Mischa, adjusting her bow.

They were interrupted by the strange sound of sizzling noise, over which a very deep voice droned slowly through the large black speakers situated around the stadium.

Every word echoed several times, amusing Mischa so much that she started giggling.

'Competitors to your places, please. The Marshall Singles Figure Skating Competition will commence in two minutes. Two minutes! Places please.' The announcement echoed around the stadium.

'Well he doesn't sound all that excited about this competition' thought Delia, aloud.

'Delia, are you sure that we will be able to skate?' whispered Chiko, nervously, as he prepared to go over to the competitors stand with Mischa.

'Trust my magic, and may the best man, woman, dog or bird, win.'

'First to perform' droned the voice, again, 'is Sabine Dupuis of Le Puy, France.'

The crowds cheered and welcomed the tiny brown-haired girl from France. She wore her hair in tight pigtails, tied back with gold ribbons. Her matching gold and white slinky skating costume made her look like a stumpy poodle.

Sabine scored her way through the ice with a fairly unspectacular programme. For the most part, it was made up of a few tiny jumps, but the highlight of the performance was when she landed on her bottom whilst trying to perform a double axle. She finished her programme by kneeling on the ice and pointing one finger on her chin, with a matching cheeky grin for the judges.

The crowds applauded politely. A few red roses were thrown on to the ice for her. Sabine bowed to the people and smiled graciously.

The following two competitors, both men, one from New York, America, and the other from Stockholm, Sweden, made the same amount of mistakes, but managed to get a few more cheers than the unfortunate Sabine Dupuis.

'Next, Chiko the robin, from Somerset, England.'

'Good luck' cheered Mischa, giving the robin a pat on the head.

The crowd applauded politely and whispered excitedly at the size of the robin's skates.

Chiko skated across the ice rink, unaware of the curiosity he had caused, and began his routine. He looked like a tiny pea on the vast expanse of ice, but that did not stop him from springing and jumping in the air, in time with the music. He used his wings for extra elevation and elongated jumps. As he performed, Chiko whistled along to his music, thoroughly enjoying the occasion.

After he had finished, the crowd roared wildly. TV cameras zoomed in on him and portrayed the talented Chiko on the big screens scattered around the arena. He was an instant star and favourite with the crowds. He flew around the arena, in and out of the crowd, acknowledging the applause and cheers by chirping and singing loudly.

Two small girls, wearing matching costumes, skated on to the ice and collected the red roses that were thrown from admiring ladies in the audience.

He whistled and sang with delight, having forgotten all about Daisy.

'Next' drawled the voice, even slower than before, 'Vladimir Dmitry Petrov, from Moscow, Russia.'

The tall, handsome, dark haired Russian, skated onto the rink and danced through his routine with elegance and feeling. He executed the most amazing jumps of such difficulty, but made a mistake when he tripped on a lump of ice and fell on his nose. However, he picked himself up, gracefully, and continued his programme. Vladimir sped around the ice faster and faster, taking in several jumps and executing an amazingly fast camel spin.

He ended his routine magnificently with a dazzling high jump, which enraptured the judges who stood up with applause. His skates scored through the ice as he glided to a standstill, posing with his head in the air and his arms behind his back.

When he finished, the crowds went into an uproar. 'Hooray for Vladimir.' 'Marvellous performance, magnificent!' 'He must surely be the winner.'

Russian flags waved frantically around the stadium, accompanied by loud cheering. Several bouquets of flowers were thrown on to the ice. The two small girls returned, quickly collecting flowers and small gifts that were thrown there for Vladimir.

After the uproar had quietened, the white noise reverberated around the stadium, once more.

'Finally' droned the voice, 'Mischa Jennings, from Somerset, England.'

Mischa skated onto the ice, with her silver dress, floating. She curtseyed to the audience and waited for her music, unaware that the audience were pointing at her. 'Imagine that!' shouted a spectator, 'The robin had two ice skates, and this Shetland sheepdog is wearing four!'

She crouched on the ice and covered her head with her paws. Ravel's *La Valse* played from the speakers, and Mischa rose from the ice and started skimming across without even trying to move her legs. The crowd gasped with amazement as she skated faster and faster, executing two consecutive double axels, followed by a sit-spin.

'Hooray! Hooray for Mischa' shouted the people.

As the music got louder and louder, Mischa built up her speed once more, jumped high into the air and performed two triple salchows, followed by a quadruple toe-loop.

'Unbelievable' said Petrov, with admiration.

'Incredible' added Sabine.

She skated backwards, slowly at first, then with increasing momentum, raised her front paws, and turned suddenly into another heart-stopping jump. She continued her routine, amazing the crowd with her fluid movements and stunning gracefulness on the ice. Mischa started her finishing piece by skating faster and faster around the whole rink and then going to the centre, spinning.

'No, no! The dog is attempting a beillmann spin' squeaked a small Chinese girl.

Mischa spun faster and faster on one hind leg, with her other hind leg held high above her head. The spin was so fast, it was as though she was trying to drill

her way through the ice. Finally, she finished her routine by throwing herself, belly first, onto the ice, sliding to a stop.

There was rapturous applause from the audience.

'This dog must be the world's greatest!' cheered the crowds, standing up to applaud Mischa. There was a terrific amount of noise and celebration. Many bunches of flowers, and indeed a small teddy bear, were thrown onto the ice that five small girls, in matching blue costumes, had to skate around the rink to pick them up. The first four girls handed Mischa the flowers. The fifth girl handed Mischa the teddy. Her large black eyes stared blankly through the sheltie.

Quite as expected, Mischa skated off with first prize, and Delia and Chiko helped her carry the wicker basket of goodies.

When Mischa awoke the following morning, she could not help but wonder if she had actually skated, or if it was all a dream. She scrambled out of bed and hurried into the living room to find Mrs. Jennings.

'Mischa! You lazy girl! Don't you know that it is eleven-thirty?!' Mrs. Jennings looked closely at the sheltie. 'Are you sick? Let me look at your eyes. Ooh you do look tired, as though yer've been up all night long. Come on. Oi'll make yer some brekkies with Bowzers chicken-flavoured kibble.

Just then, the doorbell rang and Mischa followed Mrs. Jennings to the front door.

It was the postman. He handed Mrs. Jennings a huge wicker basket of fruit, chocolate, sweets and cakes. It was bursting with goodies.

'For me?!' spluttered Mrs. Jennings. 'Anonymous?! Good gracious! Oi wonder who sent this. Thank yer very much!' said Harriet, blushing madly. She looked at the cellophane wrapped basket, hardly daring to believe her eyes.

She closed the door and placed the basket on the table, looking disbelievingly at it. 'There isn't even a note from the sender.' She scratched her head in amazement. 'Mischa, ha' yer got any idea who sent this lovely basket?'

'Yes! Yes!' barked Mischa. 'I won an ice skating competition, last night! I can skate. It wasn't a dream after all. Good. Good!' With that she danced around the living room, and jumped in the air to execute a triple lutz.

Bang.

She fell on the floor in a heap.

'How can you fall over your own paws?' laughed Mrs. Jennings.

Mischa picked herself up and looked towards the French window. There, pressing their nose and beak against the glass, sat Chiko and Delia, hooting with laughter.

'Oh dear. I'm so tired' sighed Mischa. 'I think I'll have a nice, long snooze.'

'Mischa, wake up. Don't you want a chocolate?' asked Mrs. Jennings, holding up a large strawberry cup in front of her nose.

'No thanks' she panted, sleepily. 'After all of that gallivanting last night, I'd better have a nap to regain my strength for tonight's performance for my fans.'

She rolled onto her back, paws in the air, and fell asleep.

'Mischa! Yer lazy pup!' said Mrs. Jennings, shaking her head as she carried her cup of tea to the dining table. She opened the cellophane and looked at the luxurious foods inside the basket.

Buried under the delicious goodies, was the teddy. Headless.

Chapter 8: Cattacitus A. Timmins

'Psst. Psst.'

Mischa continued to snore.

'Mischa! Wake up! Wake up! Wake up!'

Mischa sat up with a worried expression on her face. She gingerly opened one eye and almost fell out of her bed in fright. There, right in front of her, squirmed the largest, fattest, grubbiest mouse, that she had ever seen in her life.

In fact, his body was so huge, he looked like a dirty tennis ball with tiny arms and legs sticking out. His belly was enormous. His wildly curling tail stuck out at an angle, and his face, with pointed nose, large pink ears, and beady black eyes, stared angrily at her. He rubbed his nose with the back of his hand and cleared his throat, loudly.

'I say' said Mischa, crossly, as she got used to the idea of an extraordinarily large mouse staring at her, 'Don't you know that this is my siesta?'

'Siesta, nap, laziness. It's all the same to me' answered Boris, the mouse, in a grumpy tone. 'However, your presence is required, immediately.'

'By whom?' growled Mischa, getting more frustrated with each second of sleep lost.

'Cattackitus A. Timmins' replied the Takoda.

'What, the giant sized cat?' Mischa rambled on. 'Why does he need to see me? I don't even like cats. Well, some cats I suppose. Delia is cool, but Tizzy is stinky. A giant sized cat. Hmmm, I doubt if he wants me to catch a beach ball sized mouse like you. Now let me think, why else would he want to see me? Does he need me to play Frisbee?'

'Move! Now! Cattackitus A. Timmins, ruler of Aurora, needs to see you and all of his subjects at his Palace, immediately! Be quick to get to the Tamarix. You must not keep him waiting.'

'Well, does this great cat of Aurora know that I cannot miss my afternoon nap?' grumbled Mischa.

'Cattackitus A. Timmins, should not be kept waiting' rattled the mouse, shaking his grey head in frustration.

'Is he in the garden?' said Mischa, stretching herself extremely slowly and annoying the mouse even further.

'No! Why don't you listen you silly dog. I said Cattackitus A. Timmins wants to see you in his palace, as soon as possible' answered the mouse, furiously hopping from one foot to the other, curling his tail around his finger in impatience.

'And how am I supposed to get to this palace? Fly? Magic carpet? Skateboard?'

'Skateboard?! Just follow me, Mischa.' He gritted his teeth and wondered why he, of all the subjects of Cattackitus A. Timmins, was chosen to do this tedious job.

Mrs. Jennings walked into the kitchen.

'Eeh' screamed Mrs. Jennings, jumping up onto the brown wooden chair, surprisingly fast for such a large lady. 'Mischa. Mischa! Look at that creature! A rat! Eeh! A huge rat with a huge belly! Get it out of here, Mischa. Get it out, now! Oi knew Oi shouldn't have left the backdoor open!'

'Not again' grumbled Boris, shuffling his feet and wishing the ground would swallow him up.

'Mischa, get that thing out of my kitchen. Now!' screamed Mrs. Jennings.

'Thing? Thing?!' shouted Boris, dancing with rage.

'Follow me please, Mr. Mouse' said Mischa' leading the way towards the backdoor.

'It's Boris. Call me Boris. If you'd got up when I told you to, ten minutes ago, I wouldn't be in this compromising position' he muttered, angrily.

'Come along. This way.' Mischa pushed open the backdoors with her snout and led him down the garden path towards the Tamarix.

Mrs. Jennings jumped off the chair and ran to the backdoor, slammed it shut and bolted it. Then she opened the window and waved at Mischa. 'Good girl! Well done for getting rid of that rat. Great girl, Mischa.' She mopped her brow with her blue and white checked hanky, relieved to be rid of the vermin.

'Ooh. Oi could do with a cuppa' Harriet Jennings muttered out aloud with a quivering voice.

'Rat? Rat! Next Mrs. Jennings will call me a guinea pig' grumbled Boris.

The mouse scurried down the garden, closely followed by Mischa.

Under the Tamarix tree, they found Delia, Chiko and Daisy; Jake and Josh, the twin black cats from the bakery; and four magpies, Lucy, Lucky, Laurie and Libby, who lived in Mr. Barrowclough's orchard.

'What took you so long' hissed Delia to Boris.

'Can't you guess?' laughed the Chiko, cheekily.

'Sometimes I wonder if I'll ever be able to have my afternoon nap. I must have missed at least seven' frowned Mischa.

'Don't be silly. You sleep far too much' tittered Chiko. 'And if you still want to go back to bed, then you should ask Delia to change you into a bear, so that you can hibernate for winter.'

Mischa snatched a buttercup from the lawn and hurled it at Chiko.

'Oh stop this nonsense!' exclaimed Delia. 'Our Master awaits us.'

They arranged themselves under the Tamarix as best as they could. Delia held up her paws and recited the magic spell:

'Magic, magic, in the air,
Carry us far to the Palace, fair,
To greet our Master in his House
To hear his words, and not those of this Mouse!'

After what seemed to be a long, bumpy journey, they found themselves inside a large, beautiful lavender house.

Everything smelled of flowers. From the ceiling hung huge bouquets of roses, and foxgloves, all of different shades and sizes. Several crystal vases were dotted around the room, filled with lilies, dahlias and honeysuckle. The whole room was ablaze with colour.

Mischa looked up at the ceiling and around the room, taking in all the smells and colours. Even the chandelier was made from hundreds of trailing nasturtiums, with each flower holding a glowworm, to throw a warm light.

Bright paintings of various Takoda, wearing Mayoral chains, hung within golden frames, on the walls. Faeries, dressed in pale-blue shimmering dresses, flitted across the room, adding finishing touches to the hairstyles of the beautifully clad animals, who were dressed in fancy ball gowns and tuxedos.

'This' said Delia, extending her paws, 'is the Dressing Room.'

Delia, Daisy, Chiko and Mischa were escorted into a large silver wardrobe, studded with diamonds, by a young raccoon.

They came out clothed in the finest attire imaginable. Chiko was draped in a black, three-piece suit with silver buttons on his waistcoat. He wore a black top hat and a tiny silver ring on one claw.

Delia wore a rich red gown, with very large leg-of-mutton sleeves, and a high lace collar. Mischa's dress, a pale-green embroidered ball gown, had cream sleeves and cream lace around the edges. Daisy's gown was mauve, with golden smocking running throughout the material. The ishta wore elegant, beautiful stoned tiaras on their heads, which glistened and sparkled magnificently.

'Gosh! You do look nice, Chiko' said Mischa, admiring his top hat and ring.

Chiko cocked his head, this way and that, and yet somehow, the hat remained on his head without falling off!

Boris appeared at the door of the purple wardrobe with Josh, Jake and the four magpies, all equally well dressed in gowns and tuxedos. Boris was robed in a navy pinstriped suit, adorned by a large pocket watch attached to his white waistcoat by chain.

'It's time for us to leave for the Palace, and to listen very carefully to the wise

words of Cattackitus A. Timmins.' Boris bowed to the guests and beckoned them with his chubby hand.

He led them down a long avenue of delicate, butterfly shaped conifers. Surrounding these trees were thousands upon thousands of the most stunning rose bushes. These were so bright, glowing in the brightest shades of orange, that the roses created the impression that the avenue was on fire. In the distance, starting out very softly but growing louder and louder with every step, they heard the sounds of an orchestra playing very stately music.

'We're almost there' whispered Boris.

When they reached the their destination, the friends gasped in amazement. They faced a magnificent palace, with ice-cream cone shaped towers, covered with sapphires. The palace walls were studded with precious stones of all colours, which glittered and winked at the guests. Mischa stared with her mouth wide open.

A long, royal blue carpet led to the extraordinary large oak doors. The awestruck friends entered the palace and were kindly greeted by the guards and waiting staff of Cattackitus A. Timmins. When the guests were seated, in comfortable blue velvet chairs, laid out in theatre style, a grand flourish of trumpets sounded.

'And now' called a grey weasel at the top of his voice, 'Please stand for the great Cattackitus A. Timmins, ruler of Aurora.'

The many hundreds of chairs that filled the room scraped backwards as the guests scrambled to their feet. Cattackitus A. Timmins entered the Banquet Room, with strong, forceful steps, and took his place on stage, in front of the waiting audience.

The guests in the Banquet Room fell silent, instantly, and stared with great awe at C.A.T.

Cattackitus' presence was acknowledged by a synchronous bow from the audience.

'Please be seated, thank you.' The commanding C.A.T paused and looked around the room.

'Today' he boomed, in his deep bass voice, 'I thank you for attending this feast. I must especially thank my staff for doing their jobs so very well, both in the gardens and in the palace. The secret to our success, is in the details.' He paused to take a deep breath. 'However' turning from side to side to view the room, 'there is a situation arising.' With these words, every pair of eyes in the room glued themselves to C.A.T. 'Trouble is brewing. The Wild Cats of Drangan have been seen misusing magic for their own gratification, and are believed to be plotting to take over Aurora.'

Again, he stopped to take a breath and to observe the faces staring incredulously at him.

'It is our duty to be vigilant, and to watch out for these Wild Cats.' 'We must' he continued, 'protect our Human-Being pets, our livelihoods and our lands.'

A murmur rippled around the Banquet Room.

Cattackitus A. Timmins raised his paw for silence.

'The Wild Cats of Drangan look very similar to the average cat. However' he stopped and stared around the room once more, 'these cats have purple eyes.'

Another ripple of comments circulated around the room.

'We must contain these cats, without falsely accusing the innocent.'

'It is hoped' he stopped, turning his head to acknowledge Delia, 'that Ms. Delia Deveraux Barrowclough will formulate an antidote, with the intended capacity to erase the memories of these Wild Cats, allowing them a fresh start in our society.'

A great chatter and finger pointing at Delia took place. Mischa swelled with admiration for her favourite cat, and her best friend. She beamed at Chiko. 'I always knew that she was a clever Cat!'

Chiko nodded.

'Presently, these Wild Cats of Drangan have travelled Ireland, found their way to Scotland, and have now spread throughout England and Wales. They create havoc by turning friendly cats into our worst nightmare. We must find the ruler of the Wild Cats in order to destroy their leadership. These Wild Cats of Drangan have infiltrated Takoda and their Human-Being pets, and have even killed.' C.A.T. paused to stare around the Banquet Room.

'After the banquet' bellowed C.A.T., 'When you all return to your homes, I ask you all to exercise extreme vigilance. Not for one day, one week or one month, but constantly.' he drew a deep breath. 'These Wild Cats of Drangan are casting spells on Takoda and Human-Being pets, making them do evil deeds, and generally bring terror into every neighbourhood, every village and every city. If you come across a Wild Cat, you must notify your regional leader. There is an implementation task force in place, who will act quickly and bravely. We hope to temporarily contain the Wild Cats of Drangan by entrapping these fiends, temporarily stunning them and placing them into a deep sleep. They are to be brought back here to await Delia's antidote. Note well that these cats are extremely dangerous. Do not be tempted to corner a Wild Cat on your own.'

Cattackitus A. Timmins took a sip of melon juice from his crystal goblet. 'Regional leaders will make themselves known to you and full instructions are available from the dressing room and around the grounds.' C.A.T. stroked his whiskers thoughtfully.

'Now, the only way to restore justice and harmony is for each and everyone of you to work together, strengthen your belief in the good in our world and fight bravely, side by side with your friends. Thank you for your time and, for your attention. Fox Swing Band, please continue your excellent music, and please' he said, sweeping out his arms and embracing his audience, 'feel free to enjoy the banquet.'

Everyone ate, drank and danced all night long. Mischa danced so much that her paws were ready to fall off. Her eyes, becoming weary and droopy, shut for the night, and when she awoke, Mischa found herself under the Tamarix.

'Mischa! Mischa! Hurry on in. It's gonna rain any minute. Com'on. Hurry up, there's a storm brewing' yelled Mrs. Jennings.

Mischa raced to the kitchen, jumped straight into her basket and within a blink of an eyelid, was fast asleep.

Chapter 9: The Storm

Mischa awoke during the night to an ear-shattering blast of thunder. She ran to the living room and looked out of the French windows and into the garden. Forked lightning lit the sky. In the brief, ominous light, she thought she saw an enormous wolf-like shape. Mischa shuddered, but quickly decided that this storm should take priority over any werewolf. She quickly hid behind the sofa before the next crash of thunder rang out, vibrating the old house. The frightened sheltie placed her front paws over her ears as the loudest crack of thunder rocked her home.

Mrs. Jennings turned on the lights and ran downstairs as quickly as she could. Her normally brushed hair was standing on end as though she had had an electric shock.

'Mischa, Mischa. Are yer frightened?' She looked in the kitchen, and, seeing that the basket empty, searched for her companion.

'Mischa, where are you?'

'I'm behind the sofa, Mrs. J.' wailed the sheltie.

Mrs. Jennings saw a small snout sticking out from behind the couch. She went over to Mischa and rubbed her ears. 'This is going ta be a terrible storm. The weatherman said it's coming over from Ireland and t'will last all night. There'll be gales, rain, thunder an' lightning. Trees will be up rooted an' tiles will be blown from roofs. Our simple thatched roof won't stand a chance. We must wait out this storm in the room under the stairs. It's the safest room in th' house cos there are no windows. We'll be alright in there, my puppy.' She bent down and stroked Mischa's head. Just then a bolt of lightning struck very close to their dwelling and the house was plunged into darkness.

'Hoooowl' wailed Mischa. 'Save me, Mrs. J.'

'There there' said Mrs. Jennings, shaking as much as Mischa. 'Everythin' will be fine.'

'What about Chiko and Daisy?' wept Mischa. 'At least Delia will be in her bed in Mr. Barrowclough's kitchen.'

'There, there' said Mrs. Jennings. 'Don't worry about the storm. It'll soon pass.' She felt around for matches and candles, but only found a newspaper and her glasses case.

'The lights will come back on in no time, and then we can have a nice cup of tea and a slice of cake.'

Another ear-splitting peal of thunder roared overhead.

'Noooo' howled Mischa with her snout in the air.

There was a deep bark, followed by scratching sounds coming from the front door.

'Noooooo! A really bad storm and a werewolf!'

Mrs. Jennings grabbed onto the furniture and found her way out of the living room and to the front door.

'Don't leave me, Mrs. J.' cried Mischa.

She heard the key turn in the front door lock, and the sound of the door hinges creaking open under the force of the gales. Mischa heard the sounds of torrential rain pouring down, and the sound of heavy panting.

She lay down as unexposed as possible, quivering, and hoped that the werewolf would not find her.

The front door slammed shut as a violent gust of wind blasted through the house.

'Ooh! The werewolf has attacked Mrs. J. and I'm next.'

She crawled out from behind the sofa, on her belly, intending to make her way to the room under the stairs.

Suddenly, a huge shower of muddy water cascaded over her and around the living room.

'Eeh! The stench! Mrs. Jennings, where are you? What is this?' cried Mischa.

'Woof woof.' Mischa was greeted with a big, wet, slobbery kiss on the nose.

'Rayden? Rayden? Is that you?' Mischa stuck out her paw and felt the soggy woolly head and body of the drenched Old English sheepdog.

'It's me, you big poodle! Mrs. Jennings is fine.' Rayden sat his huge rump on the carpet and scratched his back.

'There you are, Rayden' said Mrs. Jennings, shining a watery light, from a very weak torch. 'Oi found a tea towel for you, my love. Let me dry you off.' She rubbed his head and back vigorously with the towel.

Mischa sniffed, sniffed the aroma of the old English sheepdog's wet, muddy smell. She screwed up her nose in disgust.

'Yer poor thing! Fancy! Yer were stuck out in tha' storm and not with Mr. Braithwaite. You could catch yourself a death.'

The gales rattled the house, and constant lightning continued to flash eerily around the room.

'Now come with me, both of ye. We'll have to go to the room under the stairs. There are no windows in it an' it's the safest room in the house.'

Mrs. Jennings led the two dogs to the room under the stairs and closed the door.

The three of them sat down on some worn rugs and looked at each other through the faint torchlight.

'Now, we'll have to try an' get some sleep an' wait out this storm in this little room. We can't do any more.' said Mrs. Jennings, patting both furry heads.

Mischa sniffed Rayden's smelly coat again and shuddered in disgust. It was even smellier than the cat food Ms. Amelia left outside for Tizzy.

Rayden shifted himself closer to Mischa and made himself comfortable. Mischa, meanwhile, closed her eyes and put her paws over her nose, to try and eliminate the smell of wet fur coming from the hairy Old English sheepdog.

'Now, isn't this the finest!' Mrs. Jennings found a bag of old clothes and lay her head on it, trying to sound cheerful. 'It's better in this room. We can't hear the gales and the thunder and we can't see the lightning.'

Mischa agreed, and Rayden licked her nose.

'Ger-off' said Mischa, wiping her nose with her paw.

It was a long and uncomfortable night. The thatched house took a battering from the gales. After five hours of snatches of sleep, Mrs. Jennings got up very slowly and opened the door. She walked stiffly towards the kitchen.

The dark night had transformed into a dull, grey, rainy, and very windy morning, but at least the thunder and lightning had stopped.

She opened the door to the room under the stairs. 'Com'on yer two. Thank goodness the house is still standing. We don't seem to have any leaks, but we might have to have the thatch looked at.'

Mischa and Rayden entered the kitchen and eagerly licked their lips as Mrs. Jennings got a box of "Bowzers" kibble out of the cupboard. 'It's turkey an' duck flavour. Is that alright my lovelies?'

'Yes! Yes!' they barked back, vigorously wagging their tails.

'An' after that, yer can have some tea an' a slice of me rhubarb pie.'

'Mmmm' drooled Rayden. 'Mr. Braithwaite never has pie. It's always plain rich tea biscuits. You're very lucky.' He sat on his hind legs and begged for Mrs. Jennings, and for his efforts, was rewarded with an extra bowl of Bowzers.

They wolfed down their food, and after they were satisfied, trotted around to the French Windows and peered out into the garden. In the dull grey light, they could see flowerpots, soil and bedraggled plants strewn around the garden. One of the apple trees had been uprooted and lay in a heap on top of the rhubarb patch. The patio looked like a huge, muddy swimming pool.

Rayden shook his woolly head. ''Tis a shame, but' he turned and stared into Mischa's eyes, 'Something far worse has happened.'

Mischa's eyes grew wide with fear.

'The Wild Cats of Drangan have been seen in this neighbourhood. Charlie isn't in Dr. Sort U Out's veterinary hospital because of a virus. He was attacked by Wild Cats.'

Mischa gasped in disbelief.

'And because he held out so very bravely, for such a long time, Charlie was bombarded with their evil magic. So much so, he became unconscious.' Rayden sighed. 'He's still at Doctor Sort U. Out's practice.'

Mischa nearly died with fright. 'But, we're in deepest Somerset! How can those cats be in the West Country? How have they found us?'

'Magic my girl. Bad magic.' Rayden put his fluffy paw on Mischa's shoulder. 'I'll protect you. Besides, Delia is our regional leader. Her antidote is nearly ready, and it will save Takoda and Human-Being pets.' 'Hopefully' he muttered to himself.

Later, when the rain had stopped, Mrs. Jennings, together with Mischa, took Rayden back to his home on the next street. Mr. Braithwaite was delighted to have his big, furry friend back.

'My Baby! Oi thought Oi'd lost yer in th' storm.' He hugged the huge dog, and Rayden licked his face, enthusiastically.

Mischa sniggered. 'My Baby!' she mimicked back.

'When Oi looked 'round an' seen th' damage done by tha' storm, with all tho' trees down, we're lucky to still have roofs over our heads. Oi says to me-self, Jim Braithwaite, yer lucky to be alive.'

Mrs. Jennings agreed. 'Tha' lightning and thunder, t'was terrifying. Oi thought me thatch roof was goin to blow clean away. Thank goodness Oi had Rayden and Mischa to keep me sane. Did yer see the damage at Charlotteville? The house took a bolt of lightning, making a huge hole in their roof, an' now they are mopping up the rain damage. Thank heaven nobody was killed.'

'Poor Madeleine' said Mischa, shaking her head. 'Her basket was ruined.'

'Thank yer for bringing back my baby, Harriet. Thank yer so much.'

Mr. Braithwaite waved good-bye to Mrs. Jennings.

'Bye, Mischa. Be vigilant' woofed Rayden, as he accompanied his Human-Being pet to the front door.

'Yes I will' answered Mischa.

Later that day, Mischa made her way down the muddy garden, her paws sinking into the soggy grass with every step. She found Chiko perched on the battered laburnum tree.

'Where did you sleep last night? Were you afraid? Where did Daisy sleep? I was very worried about you both.'

Chiko cocked his head to one side and smiled. 'Daisy and I flew down Mr. Barrowclough's chimney, and we spent the night at Delia's house.'

'Did someone mention my name?' meowed Delia, tiptoeing through the mud, shaking each paw in turn trying to ditch the stodgy, sticky mess.

'Delia, Chiko!' said Mischa excitedly. 'Rayden stayed at my house last night, and he said that the Wild Cats have been seen in Midsomer-Atte-Stoke *and* that they attacked Charlie!'

'Shh' hissed Delia, looking around cautiously. 'It's true. But we must try to contain terror and gossip amongst the smaller Takoda.'

'Charlie is out of danger. I managed to remove some of the bad magic. For the moment, he's having a well-earned rest at Dr. Sort U. Out's, and will eventually make a full recovery.' Delia jumped onto a straggled laburnum branch.

'Everyone is responsible for guarding his or her own gardens, front and back. We will have to take turns patrolling the streets of the village. Rayden, Willow, Biggles, Mac and Honey are walking their Human-Being pets every evening between 1 and 6pm, for one hour each. Mischa, you are to take Mrs. Jennings for a walk at 6pm. Chiko and I will patrol the streets at 7pm. Jake and Josh are watching the backs of gardens which do not have Takoda. Claude, Sammy, Poppy, Cheyenne and Bruno are also on watch-out alert.' Delia took a breath. 'If you see a strange cat, always report it, even if it does not have purple eyes.' She nodded wisely. Whatever happens, do not approach strange cats on your own.' Delia looked up at the sun, and like a trained explorer, knew that it was past high noon. 'Good. The first patrol is now taking place.'

Suddenly, a shriek and a yell came from the other side of the street. Chiko and Delia looked at each other meanwhile Mischa raced immediately in the direction of the commotion.

'That's Claude' said Delia. 'Come on.'

There was a long, deep, yip, yip, yowl. Chiko and Delia made it to Claude's house to find the cream, woolly terrier, assisted by Mischa, pinning down a spitting, hissing, angry cat. Delia scattered herbal dust onto the cat, and sent it into a deep sleep.

'Good! This Wild Cat is neutralised. It's been made safe, at least temporarily.'

There was another 'yip, yip, yowl' coming from the direction of Poppy's house.

'A two pronged attack! The two of you stay here and watch this cat while I go and check out the alarm.'

Delia ran towards the barking and jumped over the side gate and into Poppy's garden. From here, she could see Poppy and Honey, pinning down another purple-eyed cat. Delia sprinkled it with the same herbal powder that she had developed, earlier. The Wild Cat fell into a deep sleep.

The two sleeping Wild Cats were dragged by their capturers to the Tamarix, and were here met by Delia and Chiko.

'We must act quickly and quietly. We do not want to surprise any more Wild Cats.'

The Tamarix shook some of her gentle feathery flower dust on to the Takoda below.

Delia enchanted another spell, and they magically travelled to the palace grounds.

'Hooray' cried the Takoda of the palace, when they first cast eyes on the two Wild Cats. 'In total, we've now captured twenty-seven cats! Delia, is your antidote ready?'

'I will need another few minutes. Will you please gather all of the Wild Cats, so that I can treat them quickly.'

Delia left for her workshop, and returned half an hour later with a large vial of glowing, green liquid.

'That looks like the stuff Mrs. J. uses to wash my bowl' whispered Mischa to

Honey. Mischa sniffed Rayden's coat, 'suppose he could do with some as well' and laughed.

Rayden looked down his long white snout at Mischa, with his large hazel eyes covered by three strands of hair. 'Mischa, my only gal. You can scrub my back anytime.'

Mischa blushed and fell backwards with fright, which Poppy found very amusing.

Delia walked from one sleeping cat to the next, giving each Drangan cat three drops of green solution from the vial.

Slowly, the cats awakened, and began to meow plaintively, crying for food. Their purple eyes returning to their normal shades of green.

'It's working' sighed Delia. 'They shouldn't remember a thing. However, these are only pawns in this escapade. We must find the leader of the Wild Cats of Drangan.'

They reappeared under the Tamarix, and were about to plan the next patrols when they heard a mixture of whistling and shrieks from Chiko, Daisy and the four magpies.

'Quick, more Wild Cats' hissed Delia. 'Chiko, fly into my garden and see if there are any Wild Cats. Mischa, take the left side of the house, and I'll take the right. If you spot a cat, give two yips and a yowl.'

They nodded and split up, quickly and quietly.

Mischa found Mrs. Jennings and Mr. Barrowclough standing perfectly still, as if they had been set in cement! Mrs. Jennings had been gesturing with her hand, and it was still suspended in mid-air. Mr. Barrowclough had been scratching his ear, and his arm was bent upwards and over, like a ballerina. Their eyes were unfocused.

Mischa put her paw over her mouth in horror. 'Don't worry Mrs. J. I'll save you' she whispered, 'but first I must catch that Wild Cat.'

The brave sheltie crept around the garden, and on coming to the log supply tucked away in one corner, she saw a cat's tail sticking out.

She jumped onto the back of the ferocious Wild Cat, pinning it to the ground, and let out two yips and a yowl.

The savage cat spat at Mischa, and scratched the sheltie with its menacing claws. Mischa, severely startled, allowed the Wild Cat to escape her clutch. However, quickly picking herself back up, she raced to the cat, throwing herself at its neck. They rolled over and over, Mischa clinging to the cat for dear life. Delia and Chiko charged over, and using her herbal powder, Delia subdued the spitting, hissing animal.

'Oh gosh' squealed Mischa. 'It's Tizzy! I guess we now know why we always thought that there was something wrong with that cat. Help her Delia, please.'

'Yes' replied Delia, quietly. 'Tizzy was behaving strangely, and so it has come to this.'

Delia returned to Mrs. Jennings and Mr. Barrowclough and shook more feathery flowers, and orange dust from her herbal collection. She raised her paws, and shook the Human-Bing pets, quietly reciting to herself with eyes closed, tightly.

The two Human-Being pets returned back to themselves, apparently with no recollection of what had just happened.

'Mr. Barrowclough, wha' a lovely surprise. Fancy seeing yer in my garden!' said Mrs. Jennings with a doubtful expression on her face.

Mr. Barrowclough scratched his head, and then his chin. He looked at Mrs. Jennings, turned around and looked over the fence into his own garden. Turned around three times, and scratched his head again. 'Funny, tha' Harriet. Oi can't remember what happened! Oi don't know how Oi got here!'

'Come in an' have a cup of tea. Tha'll make yer feel better.' Said Mrs. Jennings wondering why on earth Brian Barrlowclough would bother climbing over the fence to be inside her garden, when he could chat quite easily from the other side.

'Do you know. Oi think Oi'll take you up on yer kind offer.' He turned around in a full circle once again, and looked about him, still not quite sure how he got into Mrs. Jennings' garden. The two of them went inside the back door, baffled and confused about what had just happened.

Tizzy was transported to the palace, and would now receive a dose of the green liquid and become her true self, once more. She would not remember the past and her stint as a Wild Cat.

Cattackitus A. Timmins was delighted. He called a great feast in the palace, and had all the Takoda of Midsomer-Atte-Stoke to attend. There were sandwiches, pastries, jellies, desserts, cakes of all descriptions, and lots of sweets and chocolates. The transformed Wild Cats, including Gizmo from the Country Café, were totally oblivious to what had happened, and they joined in the fun and dancing.

Cattackitus A. Timmins stood up for an announcement. 'Thank you, all of you, for your great work. Today we must celebrate. Evil magic has no place in our society. The main danger in Somerset is now over. All of our guests' he said, smiling at the converted Wild Cats, 'will be taken home this evening. And Fifi' he said, smiling at a small, white, lop-eared rabbit, 'will be reunited with her Human-Being pet. I congratulate all of you' he added, directed to the smallest mouse sitting on a red jelly on a table in the corner. 'To celebrate today's success, our own Fox Swing Band will play dance music in to the evening.'

The palace erupted into cheers and merriment. Mischa scurried across the dance floor to Zac, the goat, who was the best dancer. After dancing with him for fifteen minutes, the sly red fox, who played double bass in the swing band, grabbed Mischa and kissed her nose.

'Well done, Mischa' he smiled. 'I heard you were very brave.' Mischa blushed for the second time that day.

The Takoda continued dancing, drinking melon juice and eating delicious food, well into the early morning.

Later that day, when the streets had been cleared of the storm debris, and life in Midsomer-Atte-Stoke had finally returned to some kind of normality, Mrs. Jennings removed three freshly baked banana cakes from the oven. The rich, warm aroma of the moist cakes was sumptuous. Mischa licked her lips. 'Ooh, I can't wait for a slice of that cake' she panted. She sat up on her hind legs and waved her front paws.

'Yes, Mischa. Oi know you want some of me cake, but yer'll have ta wait until it's cooled down.' She put the kettle on the ancient range cooker for her umpteenth cup of tea that day.

'Oi've made extra cakes, today. One fer you, Mac and Rayden.'

Mischa shuddered at the thought of sharing a cake with Mac.

Mrs. Jennings took her tea and cake into the living room, and was just about to sit down and enjoy it, when she heard sounds coming from the front garden, next door. Harriet went over to the window and pulled the curtain across. 'Ah, bless her. There's Ms. Amelia struggling with her walking frame.' She sighed loudly. 'Ah, Mischa. She's so frail and ill looking. Oi'll go over and give her one of those cakes.'

She returned to the kitchen to wrap one of the banana cakes in greaseproof paper, headed to the front door and walked over to Ms. Amelia's garden. 'Let me help you' said Mrs. Jennings, kindly, as the frail lady struggled to put a small bag of rubbish in the bin.

'Ooh, thank yer so much, Harriet. My fingers are getting stiffer and I'm less able to cope, these days.'

'Just let me know if Oi can be of any help, by doing yer shopping, yer washing, anything at all. Oi've just made banana cakes. Would you like one? It's fresh from the oven' said Mrs. Jennings, holding out the wrapped cake.

'That smells delicious. I don't know when I've last tasted fresh cake.' She stared into space, with hunger in her eyes. 'Please put it in the basket of my frame. Thank you.'

'That was a terrible storm last night, Ms. Amelia. Oi hope yer cottage wasn't damaged' said Mrs. Jennings, placing the cake inside the basket and looking upwards to Ms. Amelia's rundown cottage roof.

'Storm? Last night? I must have slept through it' said Ms. Amelia, shaking her head. 'My medication is very strong these days. I'd sleep through anything.'

'It was a very bad storm. There were trees down an' the river flooded its banks. The farm crops were ruined. An' telephone an' electricity lines were down and off for a while, too' said Mrs. Jennings, closing Ms. Amelia's gate and standing to the outside of it, looking at poor Amelia's bedraggled, weed infested garden.

The ancient black, wrought iron house sign at Ms. Amelia's gate swung to and fro, creaking and grating in sympathy with her walking frame.

'Dear oh dear' said Ms. Amelia, shaking her head. 'The weather is odd these days.' She looked across the road at strewn branches, large muddy puddles and then up, at the sky. 'Thank you for the cake, Harriet. I wish I could do more for you.' She turned and headed slowly for her front door. The walking frame creaked annoyingly. The signpost swung backwards and forwards, to and fro.

Mischa wiped a tear from her eye as she stood by the front door, watching.

'Poor Ms. Amelia' wailed Mischa. 'She's so gentle and frail, and so, so helpless.'

Mrs. Jennings returned to her front garden, removing leaves and broken branches. She picked up a bird feeder that had been tossed to the ground by the storm, and replaced it on a branch of the bald flowering cherry, which had been stripped of its beautiful blossoms. She piled the debris into a corner by the wall and shook her head at the destruction of her garden, then headed inside to make a fresh cup of tea.

Ms. Amelia walked slowly and with staggered steps, aided by her grating walking-frame, which clumped and creaked with every move. She eventually reached her aged front door and smiled.

Her eyes twinkled.
Purple.

THE END

CPSIA information can be obtained
at www.ICGtesting.com
Printed in the USA
2654LVUK00002B